65p

Reflections

AN ENGLISH COURSE
for students aged 14–18

SIMON CLEMENTS
JOHN DIXON
LESLIE STRATTA
formerly of
Walworth Comprehensive School

Illustrated by
CHARLES KEEPING

OXFORD UNIVERSITY PRESS

Oxford University Press, Ely House, London W.1

GLASGOW NEW YORK TORONTO MELBOURNE WELLINGTON
CAPE TOWN SALISBURY IBADAN NAIROBI LUSAKA ADDIS ABABA
BOMBAY CALCUTTA MADRAS KARACHI LAHORE DACCA
KUALA LUMPUR SINGAPORE HONG KONG TOKYO

Questions and exercises © Oxford University Press, 1963

FIRST PUBLISHED 1963
REPRINTED 1964 (*twice*), 1966 (*twice*), 1968, 1969

PRINTED IN GREAT BRITAIN
BY BUTLER & TANNER LTD., FROME AND LONDON

CONTENTS

CONTENTS

Questions of Our Time

A teacher's book, published separately, includes a full discussion of approaches to each topic and suggestions for further activities.

LIST OF PLATES

Each photograph was chosen for its power to suggest new understanding of human experience. The authors and publishers are grateful to the following for permission to reproduce their work:

Nos. 2, 4, 5, 6, 7, 8, 9, 11, 12, 13, 14, and 16; Roger Mayne, whose work especially has helped to educate us in the possibilities of such photography

No. 3; Euan Duff: No. 20; John Hopkins: Nos. 10, 15, 17, 18; Radio Times Hulton Picture Library: No. 1; The L.C.C. library. No. 19; Unesco.

Prayer before Birth

I am not yet born; O hear me.
Let not the bloodsucking bat or the rat or the stoat or the
   clubfooted ghoul come near me.

I am not yet born; console me
I fear that the human race may with tall walls wall me,
   with strong drugs dope me, with wise lies lure me,
      on black racks rack me, in blood-baths roll me.

I am not yet born; provide me
With water to dandle me, grass to grow for me, trees to talk
   to me, sky to sing to me, birds and a white light
      in the back of my mind to guide me.

            *   *   *

I am not yet born; O fill me
With strength against those who would freeze my
     humanity, would dragoon me into a lethal automaton,
       would make me a cog in a machine, a thing with
         one face, a thing, and against all those
           who would dissipate my entirety, would
             blow me like thistledown hither and
               thither or hither and thither
                 like water held in the
                   hands would spill me.
Let them not make me a stone and let them not spill me.
Otherwise kill me.

                              LOUIS MACNEICE

Family, Community, and Work

OLD AGE

Nightmare

An American called Simon McKeever is on his weekly trip into town from an old people's Home. He has just found a twenty-five cent piece and wants to buy himself a can of tobacco, a rare luxury for someone as poor as he is.

He never confided to his roommates that almost every night his sleep was disturbed by the same loathsome nightmare: he was on a road—a car came—he tried to move—and he was run down like a cockroach and squashed; then, most distressing of all, people stood around examining the remains and said: 'Why—he was only a cockroach after all; not a man, a bug.' He had pondered in vain over the dream; he was ashamed of it and he never spoke of it.

The nightmare was teasing his mind unpleasantly at this moment. He was standing on a street corner with a silver quarter in his pocket, the traffic light he had been waiting for had turned green—but he was fearful. He was fearful, but he was even more greedy for his can of good tobacco. He spat into the gutter suddenly, chuckled with nervousness and stepped down from the curb.

It was a wide avenue. Leaning heavily on his cane he inched his way, tiny step by tiny step, in a manner painful to see. A lank man, over six feet in height, McKeever had a wide, flat back and long shanks and a lean, flat body. Once he had covered ground with great loping strides but now, as he told himself sourly, he crawled like a tortoise. The traffic light changed before he had advanced a yard and a shiver of anxiety ran through his body. His bright blue eyes darted from side to side, little drops of water appeared at both temples and his mouth and angular chin worked with exertion.

Actually he was in no particular danger. It was a residential area and there were signs to motorists warning of a hospital. But the old man was so uneasy that when an auto passed by without waiting, he exploded in a shout of resentment. The driver had drawn over near the opposite curb and McKeever had not been menaced in the slightest but he paused in a tremble, cut the air with his walking stick and cried out, 'Fool—you're a fool!' . . . and instantly felt mortified. Rather often these days, when he was alone, McKeever muttered his thoughts aloud; and now, as he leaned on his walking stick and laboured on, a thin grin came to his lips and he began to whisper to himself with sardonic amusement: 'Take a turtle now, Simon—a stubborn, soft-brained thing. Out on the highway it goes, right between the wheels of the ten-ton trucks. Watch it now, you jackass, or you'll be seeing your father and mother and your good sister before your time.'

He was halfway across the street when a voice called from behind him, 'Going for a hike, Mr Mac?' The little nurse, who was his special friend at the clinic, was running after him. She reached him, linked her arm with his and glanced up at him flirtatiously. 'Take me along?'

Indeed he would, and he was thankful that the rest of the traffic canyon would be negotiated on her arm, but he worked his mouth in silence for a while and then replied, 'Nope, I'm not going to . . . Not taking you anywhere.' His speech was vigorous, the tone strong and faintly shaded by the Irish twist of his childhood, the words clean-spoken. 'Just a gold digger, you are . . . chasing after me like all the others. You women make me miserable.'

The nurse laughed. McKeever pressed her arm and smiled down at her.

from *The Journey of Simon McKeever* by ALBERT MALTZ

This passage suggests some of the difficulties that old people have to face. What are they?

From your own knowledge and observation, what other difficulties would you say old people have to face?

How is McKeever reacting to his difficulties?

What do you notice about the way the nurse treats McKeever? Do you think she understands his position?

How do you think someone without her training might have acted?

Grandmother

A little Russian boy whose father has just died is travelling on a boat along the great River Volga. He and his mother are being taken to their new home by his grandmother, whom he has met for the first time only a few days before. When the steamer puts in at a riverside town, the boy is left alone in his cabin and begins to feel afraid.

Gradually the bustle overhead quieted down, the steamer stopped trembling, the splashing of the water ceased. A wet wall blocked the window of the cabin; it became dark and stuffy, and the bundles seemed to swell and crowd me out. What if they left me here on this empty steamer for good?

I went to the door. It was shut tight and I was unable to turn the brass knob. I took a bottle of milk and swung it at the knob with all my force. The bottle smashed and the milk flowed over my feet and into my boots.

Crushed by my failure, I lay down on the bundles and cried myself to sleep.

When I woke up the steamer was once more trembling, the water splashing, and the window of the cabin was shining like the sun. My grandmother was sitting beside me combing her hair and frowning as she muttered something to herself. She had an amazing quantity of blue-black hair which fell thickly over her shoulders, breast and knees, sweeping down to the floor. With one hand she lifted it off

11

the floor and held it tight, while with the other she forced a coarse wooden comb through the heavy strands; her mouth was screwed up, her dark eyes flashed with anger, and her face looked little and amusing in that mass of hair.

She seemed in a bad mood today, but when I asked her why she had such long hair, her voice was as soft and friendly as it had been the day before.

'Most likely a visitation from the Lord—"Here, spend your days combing this accursed mane!" In my youth I vaunted it; in my age I curse it. But get back to sleep, child. It's early yet—the sun's scarce up.'

'I don't want to sleep any more.'

'Well don't, if you're not wanting to,' she agreed, braiding her hair and glancing at the couch where my mother lay on her back straight as an arrow. 'How did you be breaking that bottle yesterday? Speak soft.'

She had a peculiar way of singing her words that made it easy for me to remember them—words as vivid and luscious as flowers. When she smiled the irises of her dark eyes expanded and shone with an inexpressible light; her smile revealed strong white teeth, and in spite of the numerous wrinkles on her swarthy cheeks, her whole face seemed young and bright. It was spoiled only by her fleshy, red-tipped nose with its flaring nostrils. She took snuff from a black, silver-embossed box. Everything about her was dark, but through her eyes one glimpsed the warm, cheerful, unquenchable light which illumined her from within. She was stout, and so bent as to be almost hunchbacked, but she moved about with the ease and agility of a large cat. And she was just as soft as that affectionate animal.

from *Childhood* by MAXIM GORKY

What do you notice about the way the old lady treats her grandson?

Judging by the grandparents you know, would you expect her to behave as she does?

The little boy seems to be watching his grandmother very carefully, trying to work out what she is like. Do any of the things he notices give you a clear impression of her personality?

How does the boy feel towards his grandmother by the end of the passage?

Homes for the ageing

It is an inescapable fact that to most people there comes a time when failing powers of mind or body make it impossible for them to manage their daily lives without some sort of help, and despite the weakened sense of family solidarity, this help is still forthcoming in many cases from children, other relatives, or occasionally friends. When an old person or old couple gives up an independent home and becomes part of another household it does not mean that all the problems of old age are automatically solved; the problems are different, not so pressing perhaps, and their solution lies more with the younger relatives than with the older people themselves.

Caring for the aged, wherever they may be living, requires skill as well as good will. Much advice is now available for those caring for young children and babies, and there are numerous books to help mothers in bringing up their families, but as far as I know little has been written about the day-to-day care of old people. Fortunately the first essentials, sympathy and affection, are very often to be found, and will carry relatives, friends and old people a long way, but not the whole way; without these two virtues the work of caring for the old can be onerous and unrewarding.

Probably the first thing for anyone to learn who has old people to care for is the need to allow them the utmost freedom of action, to realize that their personality is still individual and that social significance is essential to happiness. It is all too easy to take the attitude that the old are past doing anything and to encourage resting and doing nothing. This is mistaken kindness, though it may be an easy way of satisfying the conscience compared with the more exacting way of continual encouragement to be active, to go out, to find worth-while occupation. The latter course, however, is much more likely to promote happiness and to forestall the troubles which may arise later on, from infirmity and apathy. 'No, Mother, you sit still and let me do it,' is too often the attitude of an affectionate daughter. At first the old lady may gently resist being put completely on the shelf, but very soon she comes to accept the fact that she is old and useless and forms a habit of inertia.

In whose ever house they live an old man or woman must have a room to themselves. They prefer to be partially independent by having a gas or electric fire, with a ring, and access to running water. This means that they can get up and make their tea at whatever time they like and not have to depend on someone else to wait on them. An old person should expect to spend a great deal of time alone and not to be always sitting in the same room as the rest of the family. Children should not be kept unduly quiet because of the grandparents, and must be able to see their own friends and to be free of observation and possible criticism.

The old person should also have regular household chores in her charge. Many old people feel that they are on sufferance, in the way, in their relatives' houses, but this is not so when they are able to take over some share of the work or to mind the children when the parents go out. I have found that cleaning the stairs is a suitable occupation, as it does not entail bending and can be done at any time without getting in the way of the housewife. I remember an old lady of 99 whose job it was and to whom it gave a great deal of satisfaction. After this age she still did a good deal of washing up and her determined activity certainly did her

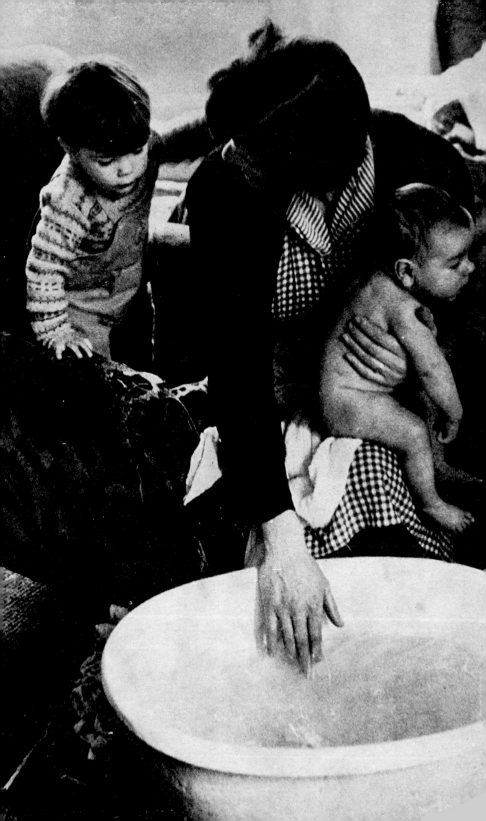

no harm as she reached the age of 103. Going slowly up and down stairs, provided they are not too steep or dark, is actually a very good form of exercise for most old people.

Besides being made to feel of value in the household old people should be encouraged to take interest in affairs outside. They should go out every day if it is reasonably fine and if their exercise can be combined with some useful purpose, so much the better; a little shopping may be done or a book changed at the library. . . . As a means of meeting other people a weekly meal or two in a restaurant is enlivening and there are clubs and church meetings to be attended. The Old People's Welfare Councils which are now established in most parts of the country, among other services arrange holidays by the sea which are of inestimable value to the old.

from *An Approach to Old Age* by MARGARET HILL

The writer suggests that the most important attitudes young relatives must have towards the old are sympathy and affection. What do you think of this? Are other qualities equally or more important?

Can you think of any mistakes that kindly relatives may make when dealing with old people?

The writer says that old people living with others prefer to be partially independent. Why do you think this is so? How may it be achieved?

What adjustments do you feel old people should expect to make when they go to live with other people?

Why do some old people tend to remain isolated or stay indoors? What can be done to encourage them to enjoy company and a life outside their home?

How do you think an old person feels when he or she is treated as unable to do anything?

Mention some of the ways individuals and the Government can and do help old people. Could more be done?

PARENTS AND CHILDREN

Early education

Some primitive people like the Manus of New Guinea are as
much at home in the water as on land. Even their houses are
built on piles above the shallow waters of the lagoons.
Imagine the problems this leads to for families with young
children. Margaret Mead describes the solutions the parents
have found.

For the first few months after he has begun to accompany
his mother about the village the baby rides quietly on her

16

neck or sits in the bow of the canoe while his mother punts in the stern some ten feet away. The child sits quietly, schooled by the hazards to which he has been earlier exposed. There are no straps, no baby harnesses to detain him in his place. At the same time, if he should tumble overboard, there would be no tragedy. The fall into the water is painless. The mother or father is there to pick him up. Babies under two and a half or three are never trusted with older children or even with young people. The parents demand a speedy physical adjustment from the child, but they expose him to no unnecessary risks. He is never allowed to stray beyond the limits of safety and watchful adult care.

So the child confronts duckings, falls, dousings of cold water, or entanglements in slimy seaweed, but he never meets with the type of accident which will make him distrust the fundamental safety of his world. Although he himself may not yet have mastered the physical technique necessary for perfect comfort in the water, his parents have. A lifetime of dwelling on the water has made them perfectly at home there. They are sure-footed, clear-eyed, quick-handed. A baby is never dropped; his mother never lets him slip from her arms or carelessly bumps his head against door post or shelf. All her life she has balanced upon the inch-wide edges of canoe gunwales, gauged accurately the distance between house-posts where she must moor her canoe without ramming the outrigger, lifted huge fragile water-pots from shifting canoe platforms up rickety ladders. In the physical care of the child she makes no clumsy blunders. Her every move is a reassurance to the child, counteracting any doubts which he may have accumulated in the course of his own less sure-footed progress. So thoroughly do Manus children trust their parents that a child will leap from any height into an adult's outstretched arms, leap blindly and with complete confidence of being safely caught.

Side by side with the parents' watchfulness and care goes the demand that the child himself should make as much effort, acquire as much physical dexterity, as possible. Every

17

gain a child makes is noted, and the child is inexorably held to his past record. There are no cases of children who toddle a few steps, fall, bruise their noses, and refuse to take another step for three months. The rigorous way of life demands that the children be self-sufficient as early as possible. Until a child has learned to handle his own body, he is not safe in the house, in a canoe or on the small islands. His mother or aunt is a slave, unable to leave him for a minute, never free of watching his wandering steps. So every new proficiency is encouraged and insisted upon. Whole groups of busy men and women cluster about the baby's first step, but there is no such delightful audience to bemoan his first fall. He is set upon his feet gently but firmly and told to try again. The only way in which he can keep the interest of his admiring audience is to try again. So self-pity is stifled and another step is attempted.

from *Growing Up in New Guinea* by MARGARET MEAD

Why do you think the Manus parents do not rely on older children or even teenagers to look after the two and three year-olds?

Do parents in your part of the world sometimes have the same feeling, and, if so, why?

The mothers constantly handle their babies with care and skill. How does this affect the babies' outlook and behaviour?

What differences can unskilful handling make to a baby's behaviour?

The way the Manus rear their children has important disadvantages for the parents. Would you say that some English parents put up with equal disadvantages? If so, describe them.

When toddlers make mistakes, do the parents you know react similarly to the Manus parents, or differently? How might parents' reactions affect their children?

The good times

Mr Morel worked in the Nottinghamshire mines at the end
of the last century. In this scene he is at home with his
young children.

The only times when he entered again into the life of his
own people was when he worked, and was happy at work.
Sometimes, in the evening, he cobbled the boots or mended
the kettle or his pit-bottle. Then he always wanted several
attendants, and the children enjoyed it. They united with
him in the work, in the actual doing of something, when he
was his real self again.

He was a good workman, dexterous, and one who,
when he was in a good humour, always sang. He had
whole periods, months, almost years of friction and nasty
temper. Then sometimes he was jolly again. It was nice to
see him run with a piece of red-hot iron into the scullery,
crying:

'Out of my road—out of my road!'

Then he hammered the soft, red-glowing stuff on his iron
goose, and made the shape he wanted. Or he sat absorbed
for a moment, soldering. Then the children watched with
joy as the metal sank suddenly molten, and was shoved
about against the nose of the soldering-iron, while the room
was full of a scent of burnt resin and hot tin, and Morel was
silent and intent for a minute. He always sang when he
mended boots because of the jolly sound of the hammering.
And he was rather happy when he sat putting great patches
on his moleskin pit trousers, which he would often do, considering them too dirty, and the stuff too hard, for his wife
to mend.

But the best time for the young children was when he
made fuses. Morel fetched a sheaf of long sound wheat-
straws from the attic. These he cleaned with his hand, till
each one gleamed like a stalk of gold, after which he cut the
straws into lengths of about six inches, leaving, if he could,

19

a notch at the bottom of each piece. He always had a beautifully sharp knife that could cut a straw clean without hurting it. Then he set in the middle of the table a heap of gunpowder, a little pile of black grains upon the white scrubbed board. He made and trimmed the straws while Paul and Annie filled and plugged them. Paul loved to see the black grains trickle down a crack in his palm into the mouth of the straw, peppering jollily downwards until the straw was full. Then he bunged up the mouth with a bit of soap—which he got in his thumb-nail from a pat in a saucer—and the straw was finished.

'Look, dad!' he said.

'That's right, my beauty,' replied Morel, who was peculiarly lavish of endearments to his second son. Paul popped the fuse into the powder-tin, ready for the morning, when Morel would take it to the pit, and use it to fire a shot that would blast the coal down.

Meantime Arthur, still fond of his father, would lean on the arm of Morel's chair, and say:

'Tell us about down pit, daddy.'

This Morel loved to do.

'Well, there's one little 'oss—we call him Taffy,' he would begin. 'An he's a fawce un!'

Morel had a warm way of telling a story. He made one feel Taffy's cunning.

'He's a brown un,' he would answer, 'an' not very high. Well, he comes i' the stall wi' a rattle, an' then yo' 'ear 'im sneeze. " 'Ello, Taff," you say, "what art sneezin' for? Bin ta'ein' some snuff?" '

'An' 'e sneezes again. Then he slives up an' shoves 'is 'ead on yer, that cadin'.

' "What's want, Taff?" yo' say.'

'And what does he?' Arthur always asked.

'He wants a bit o' bacca, my duckey.' This story of Taffy would go on interminably, and everybody loved it.

Or sometimes it was a new tale. . . .

These happy evenings could not take place unless Morel

21

had some job to do. And then he always went to bed very early, often before the children. There was nothing remaining for him to stay up for, when he had finished tinkering, and had skimmed the headlines of the newspaper.

from *Sons and Lovers* by D. H. LAWRENCE

Morel is often moody and bad-tempered. Why should he be happy in this scene?

The children are obviously enjoying the chance to help their father. Do you think they are gaining more than enjoyment?

Can you think of occasions in your experience when a child has gained something special from helping his or her mother or father?

What do you notice about the relationship between Morel and the children as he tells them the story of Taffy?

Black boy

Richard Wright, a young coloured boy, grew up in the southern states of the U.S.A. where racial feeling was strong. His mother was a widow, and he was often left to fend for himself with the rest of the gang.

Night would fall. Bats would zip through the air. Crickets would cry from the grass. Frogs would croak. The stars would come out. Dew would dampen the earth. Yellow squares of light would glow in the distance as kerosene lamps were lit in our homes. Finally, from across the fields or down the road a long slow yell would come:
  'Youuuuuuu, Daaaaaavee!'
Easy laughter among the boys, but no reply.
  'Calling the hogs.'
  'Go home, pig.'
22

Laughter again. A boy would slowly detach himself from the gang.

'Youuuuuu, Daaaaaavee!'

He would not answer his mother's call, for that would have been a sign of dependence. The boy would trot home slowly and there would be more easy laughter. More talk. One by one we would be called home to fetch water from the hydrant in the back yard, to go to the store and buy greens and meal for tomorrow, to split wood for kindling.

We were now large enough for the white boys to fear us and both of us, the white boys and black boys, began to play our traditional racial roles as though we had been born to them, as though it was in our blood, as though we were being guided by instinct. All the frightful descriptions we had heard about each other, all the violent expressions of hate and hostility that had seeped into us from our surroundings, came now to the surface to guide our actions. The roundhouse was the racial boundary of the neighbourhood, and it had been tacitly agreed between the white boys and the black boys that the whites were to keep to the far side of the round house and we blacks were to keep to our side. Whenever we caught a white boy on our side we stoned him; if we strayed to their side they stoned us.

Our battles were real and bloody; we threw rocks, cinders, coal, sticks, pieces of iron, and broken bottles, and while we threw them we longed for even deadlier weapons. If we were hurt, we took it quietly; there was no crying or whimpering. If our wounds were not truly serious, we hid them from our parents. We did not want to be beaten for fighting. Once, in a battle with a gang of white boys, I was struck behind the ear with a piece of broken bottle; the cut was deep and bled profusely. I tried to stem the flow of blood by dabbing at the cut with a rag and when my mother came from work I was forced to tell her that I was hurt, for I needed medical attention. She rushed me to a doctor, who stitched my scalp; but when she took me home she beat me, telling me that I must never fight white boys again, that I might be killed by them, that she had to work and had no time to worry about my fights. Her words did not sink in, for they conflicted with the code of the streets. I promised my mother that I would not fight, but I knew that if I kept my word I would lose my standing in the gang, and the gang's life was my life.

from *Black Boy* by RICHARD WRIGHT

The boys here have a strong loyalty to the gang. How does this affect the way they feel towards their parents?

Why might a gang be particularly important to a boy like Richard?

Do you agree with the reasons the mother gives to her son for not fighting? Do you think there are other reasons she could have given?

His mother's words 'conflicted with the code of the streets': try to show in your own words what the conflict was that the boy was experiencing.

With Richard, loyalty to his mother was not strong enough to stop him fighting. When is loyalty to parents at its strongest, in your experience?

Paul brings Clara home

Paul Morel (the boy in 'The good times') is now a young man. When he brings home Clara, she rather expects to be criticized by his mother.

Mrs Morel sat in her rocking chair, wearing her black silk blouse. Her grey-brown hair was taken smooth back from her brow and her high temples; her face was rather pale. Clara, suffering, followed Paul into the kitchen. Mrs Morel rose. Clara thought her a lady, even rather stiff. The young woman was very nervous. She had almost a wistful look, almost resigned.

24

'Mother—Clara,' said Paul.

Mrs Morel held out her hand and smiled.

'He has told me a good deal about you,' she said.

The blood flamed in Clara's cheek.

'I hope you don't mind my coming,' she faltered.

'I was pleased when he said he would bring you,' replied Mrs Morel.

Paul, watching, felt his heart contract with pain. His mother looked so small, and sallow, and done-for beside the luxuriant Clara.

'It's such a pretty day, mother!' he said. 'And we saw a jay.'

His mother looked at him; he had turned to her. She thought what a man he seemed, in his dark, well-made clothes. He was pale and detached-looking; it would be hard for any woman to keep him. Her heart glowed; then she was sorry for Clara.

'Perhaps you'll leave your things in the parlour,' said Mrs Morel nicely to the young woman.

'Oh, thank you,' she replied.

'Come on,' said Paul, and he led the way into the little front room, with its old piano, its mahogany furniture, its yellowing marble mantelpiece. A fire was burning; the place was littered with books and drawing boards. 'I leave my things lying about,' he said. 'It's so much easier.'

She loved his artist's paraphernalia, and the books, and the photos of people. Soon he was telling her: this was William, this was William's young lady in the evening dress, this was Annie and her husband, this was Arthur and his wife and the baby. She felt as if she were being taken into the family. He showed her photos, books, sketches, and they talked a little while. Then they returned to the kitchen. Mrs Morel put aside her book. Clara wore a blouse of fine silk chiffon, with narrow black-and-white stripes; her hair was done simply, coiled on top of her head. She looked rather stately and reserved.

'You have gone to live down Sneinton Boulevard!' said

25

Mrs Morel. 'When I was a girl—girl, I say!—when I was a young woman *we* lived in Minerva Terrace.'

'Oh, did you!' said Clara. 'I have a friend in number six.'

And the conversation had started. They talked Nottingham and Nottingham people; it interested them both. Clara was still rather nervous; Mrs Morel was still somewhat on her dignity. She clipped her language very clear and precise. But they were going to get on well together, Paul saw.

Mrs Morel measured herself against the younger woman, and found herself easily stronger. Clara was deferential. She knew Paul's surprising regard for his mother, and she had dreaded the meeting, expecting someone rather hard and cold. She was surprised to find this little, interested woman chatting with such readiness; and then she felt, as she felt with Paul, that she would not care to stand in Mrs Morel's way. There was something so hard and certain in his mother, as if she never had a misgiving in her life.

from *Sons and Lovers* by D. H. LAWRENCE

In her first meeting with Mrs Morel, Clara is very nervous. What might suggest this to Mrs Morel?

How would you say Mrs Morel behaves towards Clara when they are first introduced?

What do you think Mrs Morel's feelings are towards Paul?

What helps to make Clara begin to feel at home in the house?

Mrs Morel and Clara are rather on their dignity. Try to explain why both of them take up this attitude.

Judging by the last paragraph, what are Mrs Morel and Clara both doing as they talk politely to each other?

Do you feel this situation is true to life, to judge by your experience, or does it sound false?

THE HOME

Living-rooms and kitchens

Antony Bertram is an architect and before he can design a
home he has to think about what a family needs. In this
extract he discusses how space can be organized to help the
family. There is still much argument between architects
about which solution is the best.

We can begin with the living-rooms. The first consideration,
of course, is what we use our living-rooms for. In most
houses there are separate dining- and sitting-rooms, but this
is a convention that should be seriously questioned. It is no
doubt right when the house is large enough for two big
rooms, but when it is not, then it becomes a choice between
two little rooms and one big one. A small room is depressing

27

and prison-like. The single big room not only overcomes that disadvantage, but also means an immense saving of labour and firing. It is partly because of labour and firing that, where there are two rooms in a cheap house, it so often happens that the sitting-room is hardly ever used. That is less common than it was, but we have all seen those dreary dead rooms that are reserved for company. Surely it is better to have a large friendly room in daily use, with a dining-table at one end and easy chairs and so on at the other. The space can be even further freed by having a dining-table that folds away, of which there are now many designs available.

Apparently there are many people who prefer another combination, that of kitchen and dining-room. But it is very difficult to make that pleasant. I have seen satisfactory planning for it, with the dining-tables and chairs set in an alcove at the opposite end of the room from the sink and cooker; or the sink and cooker in an alcove that can be shut off with a door or curtain. But the smell of cooking and the 'atmosphere' of housework are not so easily hidden. In fact there can be little doubt that it is better to telescope the living- and dining-rooms, though it is a disadvantage of this that it reduces the chances of privacy and quiet for individuals. But there is a simple solution of that in a big enough house. Each bedroom should be furnished as a bed-sitting-room. This is perhaps the ideal—a big family room for meals, games and conversation, for the communal family life, and a bed-sitting-room for each member of the family. Electric heating has made this practical.

In furnishing a living-room from scratch a family should draw up a list of their activities in order of frequency. The things they do most often, must be most easily done. It is ridiculous how in some houses there is an orgy of discussion and furniture removal before the family can settle down to something they do constantly, to playing cards, for example. A room should be planned, not on a conventional basis, but on the habits of the family. Room-design is first and fore-

28

most the art of making the home run easily and comfortably for the family using it.

from *Design* by ANTONY BERTRAM

What kinds of rooms would you expect to find in the old conventional houses? What was each room used for?

To give greater space the author suggests it is better to combine two little rooms. What is the first combination that he suggests? What is his alternative to this?

How could the first combination be made to work?

Give two advantages of combining the functions of a room in this way.

Can you think of any advantages of combining the kitchen and dining-room? What are the two disadvantages that the author suggests? Which combination would you prefer in your home?

A large living-room can be a cheerful family room, but sometimes peace is needed. How can a quiet place be provided for each member of the family?

What practical suggestions does the author make to a family who intend to design their home from scratch?

Draw three small plans showing the three alternative combinations of rooms mentioned in this passage.

Draw a plan of an ideal living-room as you would like it.

You should have seen the mess

The following extracts are taken from a short story about a young girl called Lorna, a girl who is obsessed by dirt and untidiness and who feels that homes and offices should be ultra-hygienic.

I am seventeen years of age, and left school two years ago last month. I had my A certificate for typing, so got my first job, as a junior, in a solicitor's office. . . .

I was to start on the Monday, so along I went. They took me to the general office, where there were two senior short-hand-typists, and a clerk, Mr Gresham, who was far from smart in appearance. You should have seen the mess!! There was no floor covering whatsoever, and so dusty everywhere. There were shelves all round the room, with old box files on them. The box files were falling to pieces, and all the old papers inside them were crumpled. The worst shock of all was the tea-cups. It was my duty to make tea, mornings and afternoons. Miss Bewlay showed me where everything was kept. It was kept in an old orange box, and the cups were all cracked. There were not enough saucers to go round, etc. I will not go into the facilities, but they were also far from hygienic. After three days I told Mum, and she was upset, most of all about the cracked cups. We never keep a cracked cup, but throw it out, because those cracks can harbour germs. So Mum gave me my own cup to take to the office. . . . The next day, Saturday, I told Mum and Dad about the facilities, and we decided I should not go back to that job. Also, the desks in the general office were rickety. Dad was indignant, because Mr Heygate's concern was flourishing, and he had letters after his name.

Everyone admires our flat, because Mum keeps it spotless, and Dad keeps doing things to it. He has done it up all over, and got permission from the Council to re-modernize the kitchen. I well recall the Health Visitor, remarking to Mum, 'You could eat off your floor, Mrs Merrifield.' It is true that you could eat your lunch off Mum's floors, and any hour of the day or night you will find every corner spick and span. . . .

It so happened that I had to go to the Doctor's house, to fetch a prescription for my young brother, Trevor, when the epidemic was on. I rang the bell, and Mrs Darby came to the door. She was small, with fair hair, but too long, and a green maternity dress. But she was very nice to me. I had to wait in their living-room, and you should have seen the state it was in! There were broken toys on the carpet, and the ash trays were full up. There were contemporary pictures on the walls, but the furniture was not contemporary, but old-fashioned, with covers that were past standing up to another wash, I should say. To cut a long story short, Dr Darby and Mrs Darby have always been very kind to me, and they meant everything for the best. Dr Darby is also short and fair, and they have three children, a girl and a boy, and now a baby boy.

When I went that day for the prescription, Dr Darby said to me, 'You look pale, Lorna. It's the London atmosphere. Come on a picnic with us, in the car, on Saturday.' After that I went with the Darbys more and more. I liked them, but I did not like the mess, and it was a surprise. But I also kept in with them for the opportunity of meeting people, and Mum and Dad were pleased that I had made nice friends. So I did not say anything about the cracked lino, and the paintwork all chipped. The children's clothes were very shabby for a Doctor, and she changed them out of their school clothes when they came home from school, into those worn-out garments. Mum always kept us spotless to go out to play, and I did not like to say it, but those Darby children frequently looked like the Leary family, which the Council evicted from our block, as they were far from houseproud.

from *The Go-away Bird* by MURIEL SPARK

What is your impression of the girl's home? Does it suggest anything about her family?

What is your impression of the doctor's home and family? Which of the two homes would you prefer?

What is Lorna's attitude to other people's standards in running their homes?

How would you feel about bringing Lorna into your home? What do you think she would say about it—and would you agree with anything she said?

Do you think Lorna's own home has affected her in any way?

First room of my own

> Joe Lampton has just moved to another town to start work
> at a new job. He has found some digs and is looking at his
> room for the first time.

My room at Eagle Road was the first room of my own in the
real sense of the word. I don't count my cubicle in the
N.C.O.'s quarters at Frinton Bassett because I hardly ever
used it except for sleeping; and I always had the feeling that
it had been made impersonal by the very number of others
there before me, living on the verge of departure to another
station or death. Nor do I count my room at my Aunt
Emily's; it was strictly a bedroom. I suppose that I might
have bought some furniture and had an electric fire in-
stalled, but neither my uncle nor my aunt would have
understood the desire for privacy. To them a bedroom was
a room with a bed—a brass-railed one with a flock mattress
in my case—and a wardrobe and a hard-backed chair, and
its one purpose was sleep. You read and wrote and talked
and listened to the wireless in the living-room. It was as if
the names of the rooms were taken quite literally.

Now, following Mrs Thompson into *my room*, I was
moving into a different world. 'It's marvellous,' I said, feeling the inadequacy of the words and yet not wanting to
appear too impressed; after all, I hadn't been living in the
slums. I looked at it with incredulous delight: wallpaper
vertically striped in beige and silver, a bay window extend-
ing for almost the whole length of the room with fitted
cushions along it, a divan bed that looked like a divan and
not like a bed with its depressing daylight intimations of
sleep and sickness, two armchairs, and a dressing table,
wardrobe and writing table all in the same pale satiny
wood. On the cream-painted bookcase was a bowl of
anemones and there was a fire burning in the grate, leaving
an aromatic smell, faintly acid and faintly flower-like,
which I knew but couldn't place.

32

'Applewood,' Mrs Thompson said. 'There's an electric fire but I thought a real one would be more cheerful on a miserable day like this.'

There were three small pictures hanging on the far wall: 'The Harbour at Arles', a Breughel skating scene, and Manet's 'Olympe'. Until that day I'd never really looked at a picture. I knew, for instance, that there were three water-colours in Aunt Emily's living-room, but outside the house I couldn't even remember their subjects. I'm normally observant and I'd used the living-room daily for over two years; it was simply that in Dufton pictures were pieces of furniture, they weren't *meant* to be looked at. The Medicis quite definitely were. They belonged to a pattern of gracious living; to my surprise the worn phrase straight from the women's magazines accurately conveyed the atmosphere of the room—it was as if a ready-made suit fitted perfectly.

from *Room at the Top* by JOHN BRAINE

What had Joe disliked about living at Aunt Emily's?

Have you ever experienced similar feelings or do you think his objections were unreasonable?

Some rooms have a sort of personality. Do you think the room at Mrs Thompson's does or does it seem like a glossy magazine showroom?

Why do you think Joe felt he was moving into a different world? Have you experienced this feeling when entering a room?

Why is Joe so fascinated with the furnishings and the pictures? How important are they to a home?

Joe talks about 'gracious living'. What do you understand by this? What do you think he is getting at?

THE NEIGHBOURHOOD

The tragedy of England

Lawrence was born and brought up in the mining country
near Nottingham and he grew to realize the serious effects
that such surroundings can have upon people.

My grandfather settled in an old cottage down in a quarry-
bed by the brook at Old Brinsley, near the pit. A mile away,
up at Eastwood, the company built the first miners' dwellings—it must be nearly a hundred years ago. Now Eastwood occupies a lovely position on a hilltop, with the steep
slope towards Derbyshire and the long slope towards Nottingham. They put up a new church, which stands fine and

commanding, even if it has no real form, looking across the awful Erewash Valley at the church of Heanor, similarly commanding, away on the hill beyond. What opportunities, what opportunities! These mining villages *might* have been like the lovely hill-towns of Italy, shapely and fascinating. And what happened?

Most of the little rows of dwellings of the old-style miners were pulled down, and dull little shops began to rise along the Nottingham Road, while on the down-slope of the north side the company erected what is still known as the New Buildings, or the Square. These New Buildings consist of two great hollow squares of dwellings planked down on the rough slope of the hill, little four-room houses with the 'front' looking outward into the grim, blank street, and the 'back', with a tiny square brick yard, a low wall, and a w.c. and ash-pit, looking into the desert of the square, hard, uneven, jolting black earth tilting rather steeply down, with these little back yards all round, and openings at the corners. The squares were quite big, and absolutely desert, save for the posts for clothes lines, and people passing by, children playing on the hard earth. And they were shut in like a barracks enclosure, very strange.

So the place started. Down the steep street between the squares the Wesleyans' chapel was put up, and I was born in the little corner shop just above. Across the other side of the Square the miners themselves built the big, barn-like Primitive Methodist chapel. Along the hilltop ran the Nottingham Road, with its scrappy, ugly mid-Victorian shops. The little market-place, with a superb outlook, ended the village on the Derbyshire side, and was just here left bare, with the Sun Inn on one side, the chemist across, with the gilt pestle-and-mortar, and a shop at the other corner.

In this queer jumble of the old England and the new, I came into consciousness. As I remember, little local speculators already began to straggle dwellings in rows, always in rows, across the fields: nasty red-brick, flat-faced dwellings with dark slate roofs. The bay-window period only

35

began when I was a child. But most of the country was untouched. . . .

If the company instead of building those sordid and hideous squares, then, when they had that lovely site to play with, there on the hilltop: if they had put a tall column in the middle of the small market-place, and run three parts of a circle of arcade round the pleasant space, where people could stroll or sit, and with the handsome houses behind! If they had made big, substantial houses, in apartments of five and six rooms, and with handsome entrances. If above all, they had encouraged song and dancing—for the miners still sang and danced—and provided handsome space for these. If only they had encouraged some form of beauty in dress, some form of beauty in interior life—furniture, decoration. If they had given prizes for the handsomest chair or table, the loveliest scarf, the most charming room that the men or women could make! If they had done this, there would never have been an industrial problem. The industrial problem arises from the base forcing of all human energy into a competition of mere acquisition.

You may say that the working man would not have accepted such a form of life: the Englishmen's home is his castle, etc., etc.—'my own little home'. But if you can hear every word the next-door-people say, there's not much castle. And if you can see everybody in the square if they go to the w.c.! And if your one desire is to get out of the 'castle' and your 'own little home'!—well, there's not much to be said for it. Anyhow it's only the woman who idolizes 'her own little home'—and it's always the woman at her worst, her most greedy, most possessive, most mean. There's nothing to be said for the 'little home' any more: a great scrabble of ugly pettiness over the face of the land.

from *Nottingham and the Mining Country*
by D. H. LAWRENCE

Why do you think Lawrence felt the 'squares' inside the New Buildings were so ugly?

How would you lay out and use the central space of such a square?

Think of the houses you know and describe one of the ugliest (or least pleasant) views from their windows.

Draw a rough plan of the village in paragraph 3. What strikes you about the siting of the buildings, especially the position of the shops and market-place?

Why do you think Lawrence is so critical of 'dwellings in rows, always in rows'?

Why does Lawrence say the woman who idolizes 'her little home' is at her worst? Do you agree?

In what ways would people's lives be altered if Lawrence's proposals in paragraph 5 were carried out?

Do you agree with all of his proposals?

Blueprint for a city

Turning from the outline of the whole city, let us look at it on a smaller scale, from the point of view of the individual person in it. For although town planning is concerned with great numbers of people, and the zones where, in our multitudes, we live and work, and although we must be able to look at our cities and plan them on this large scale, it is no less concerned with small numbers of people, with the individual and his home and social circle, his daily life of work, amusement and general welfare. It is around these personal needs that the plan of the city must be built up in detail.

A city could provide a full, varied and coherent social life, and the form that a city takes can in no small measure make or mar the achievement of such a life. Our cities today prevent it by their very formlessness. They are so big that man cannot grasp them in his mind; the districts melt into one another in great, shapeless, blurred agglomerations. If he

37

lives on the fringe, perhaps his district will be distinguish-
able from the rest because it has been recently built, but it
is as likely as not that it will have no coherence, no centre,
and that it will be empty of atmosphere, a sort of negative
dormitory.

Contrast this with a small market town, for instance,
which is of a size that can be felt as a social unit, and which
has a centre intimately bound up with the lives of its inhabitants. Contrast it even with some few parts of London,
like Chelsea, Highgate, or Hampstead, which were once
villages, and which still, to this day, have a faint echo of
their former individuality. If our cities are to become good
to live in, we must regain in them this social human scale
which unplanned development has eaten up in its greedy
haste, and one way in which we could do this might be by
splitting them up into areas whose size is determined by our
everyday needs.

Cities and towns have the advantage over villages or
isolated country cottages in being able to share a large
variety of communal services. But most of our existing
cities do not share these services very well; we tend to get a
fashionable part that contains too many good things, and far
too few local centres outside it. Starting at the bottom, with
a small number of people, let us see how we could build up
a healthy and sensible structure of services and amenities in
a way that could apply to even our biggest cities.

There are some things that all of us need close to our
homes, within very easy walking distance; a few small shops
for everyday things, and a café and a pub where we can
meet our friends. And if we have babies we need a nursery
school and a creche, where we can leave them to be looked
after when we go out—for few of us are likely to have
nannies or domestic servants to keep an eye on them. About
a thousand people can support a small nursery school, so let us
suggest that a thousand people should form the smallest unit
of our city, and that this residential unit should, by the way
it is laid out, have a pleasant community feeling of its own.

There are other things that we don't need quite so often, and that we would not mind having a bit longer walk to get to. Rather bigger shops, for instance, selling the sort of things that we buy weekly and store in our homes. Several of these would make up a sociable little shopping centre, and there we would be glad of a restaurant, bigger than our local café, and capable of giving us proper meals. We would also like places of worship, a lending library, and a club or community building of some sort, where we could hold meetings and dances, play games, and produce our amateur concerts and theatricals. We also need doctors, so why not put them all together and let them share a small, but properly equipped, health and treatment centre? And we need schools, both junior and senior; often nowadays the children have to go quite a long way to their schools, crossing busy and dangerous streets, taking buses and trains. About five thousand people can support a junior and senior school that are educationally about the right size, neither too small nor too big, so let us suggest that five of our residential units should make up a neighbourhood, and share these schools and other amenities, and that this neighbourhood should also be planned in such a way that it has a coherence of its own. Such a neighbourhood would probably need offices too and might perhaps have some small local industries, like bakers and cobblers and laundries. It should certainly have a park, and it can readily be imagined that if it was planned with skill it might in itself be almost a park, with buildings set in it in groups.

But still we have not got all the services we rightly expect from town life; there are theatre and cinemas, a hospital, specialized shops, and stores where we can find almost anything. Supposing then that we make a further centre which has these three things, shared by about forty thousand people, and which with its own town hall, constitutes a borough made up of eight neighbourhoods. Here again we would need a park—quite a big one this time—and swimming baths and a railway station.

The next step up might be a whole district, made up of six boroughs, which would, in its turn, have its own centre, with a first-class technical school (the older children don't mind travelling, and can look after themselves), an exhibition hall, and a place for concerts, a bigger shopping centre, a market hall and a special hospital.

At each step in the building up of this great district, our social needs are organized so that the whole has a coherence based on local centres. It is not suggested what exact form these should take, for there are many possible ways in which it could be done, and solutions would vary according to geographical and other conditions in the locality. All that is suggested is that an underlying system of this sort could give a convenient and satisfying pattern to our cities, and that it is by no means unpractical to think that if such a pattern was taken as a long-term policy, both rebuilding and the ordinary day-to-day replacements and additions of buildings could follow it.

Perhaps a district like this is the biggest unit we should allow in our cities. Great cities might be made up of a number of them separated from one another by green belts which lead out into the surrounding countryside. All the districts would share a big entertainment, business and administration centre, to which they would be linked by a direct and rapid transport system, and would be within easy reach of the main industrial zone.

However, a pattern of this sort, which is based on our personal needs, and designed for our delight and convenience, is not in itself enough. The whole city must have its governing plan, within which the smaller patterns are details. Only a governing plan can give clarity and direction to the whole.

Published by the ROYAL INSTITUTE

OF BRITISH ARCHITECTS 1943

What individual needs do you imagine a 'negative dormitory' would fail to provide for? Do you think your area is like this or is it arranged in a helpful convenient pattern?

What does the author expect to find in a local neighbour-hood centre? Would you say your centre was better or worse than his?

A thousand people form a basic social unit, it is suggested. How can their houses and flats be laid out to give them a community feeling? Are any areas around your home laid out in this way, and do you notice any effect it has on the people living there?

Do you know of any examples in your own district or city where 'unplanned development', as the author calls it, 'has eaten up in its greedy haste . . . the social human scale'? What effects might this have on people?

Look carefully at the plan the writer suggests here for a large city or town. Would you want your town or city re-planned in this way? Give your reasons.

The writer has not mentioned buildings from previous times which are still to be found in cities. What should be done with them when the cities are being replanned? Do they make any contribution to a city?

WORK

Monday

Arthur lives in Nottingham and works in a factory. It is
Monday morning and he starts work again, after a Sunday
spent fishing.

The bright Monday-morning ring of the clocking-in machine
made a jarring note, different from the tune that played
inside Arthur. It was dead on half past seven. Once in the
shop he allowed himself to be swallowed by its diverse
noises, walked along lanes of capstan lathes and millers,
drills and polishers and hand-presses, worked by a multi-
plicity of belts and pulleys turning and twisting and slapping
on heavy well-oiled wheels overhead, dependent for power
on a motor stooping at the far end of the hall like the black
shining bulk of a stranded whale. Machines with their own

42

small motors started with a jerk and a whine under the shadows of their operators, increasing a noise that made the brain reel and ache because the weekend had been too tranquil by contrast, a weekend that had terminated for Arthur in fishing for trout in the cool shade of a willow-sleeved canal, . . . miles away from the city. Motor-trolleys moved up and down the main gangways carrying boxes of work—pedals, hubs, nuts and bolts—from one part of the shop to another. Robboe the foreman bent over a stack of new time-sheets behind his glass partition; women and girls wearing turbans and hairnets and men and boys in clean blue overalls, settled down to their work, eager to get a good start on their day's stint; while sweepers and cleaners at everybody's beck and call already patrolled the gangways and looked busy.

*　　　　*　　　　*

The minute you stepped outside the factory gates you thought no more about your work. But the funniest thing was that neither did you think about work when you were standing at your machine. You began the day by cutting and drilling steel cylinders with care, but gradually your actions became automatic and you forgot all about the machine and the quick working of your arms and hands and the fact that you were cutting and boring and rough-threading to within limits of only five thousandths of an inch. The noise of motor-trolleys passing up and down the gangway and the excruciating din of flying and flapping belts slipped out of your consciousness after perhaps half an hour, without affecting the quality of the work you were turning out, and you forgot your past conflicts with the gaffer and turned to thinking of pleasant events that had at some time happened to you, or things that you hoped would happen to you in the future. If your machine was working well—the motor smooth, stops tight, jigs good—and you sprung your actions into a favourable rhythm you became happy. You went off into pipe-dreams for the rest of the day. And in the evening,

43

when admittedly you would be feeling as though your arms and legs had been stretched to breaking-point on a torture rack, you stepped out into a cosy world of pubs and noisy tarts that would one day provide you with the raw material for more pipe-dreams as you stood at your lathe.

from *Saturday Night and Sunday Morning*
by ALAN SILLITOE

What are the things that affect Arthur as he enters the factory?

Do you think many factories are rather like this?

Can you understand his choice of fishing for the week-ends?

Robboe is a strange name: it might be short for 'Robinson' but might also suggest something about the foreman. Can you think what this may be?

Why do you think Arthur, while he is at the factory, forgets the machine and his work?

Arthur forgets his work once he is outside the factory. Is this understandable? Has all work this effect on people?

What effects has Arthur's work on the sort of life he lives outside the factory?

Can you think of other people whose lives are strongly affected by their work?

White-collar girl

This is the story (according to the author) of what happens to many American girls who want to go and work as typists in a big city.

In American folklore, the white-collar girl is usually born of lower middle-class parents. High school plays an important part in the creation of her rather tense personality. She

44

may take a commercial course in high school, and possibly a
year or two of business college. Upon graduation, being
smart and pretty, she gets a job in her own town. But she
yearns for independence from family and other local ties;
she wants to go to the big city, most of all New York. She
leaves home, and the family becomes of secondary importance, for it represents a restriction on independence. Going
home to see the folks is a reluctantly done chore, and she
can't wait to get back to the big city. . . .

The white-collar girl has a close friend, sometimes from
the same home town, and usually a girl more experienced
in the big city. They commonly share an apartment, a
wardrobe and a budget, their dates and their troubles. The
close friend is an essential psychological need in the big city,
and the white-collar girl's only salvation from loneliness
and boredom.

The first job is a continuation of her education as a steno-
grapher or typist. Her pay check is small, but she does learn
office routine with its clean, brisk, new, efficient bustle. She
also learns how to handle the male element in the office.
She laughs about small, funny incidents with the other girls,
especially last night's date and tonight's. She is given her
first cocktail by a salesman who is an expert in the psychology of girl stenographers.

The first job is usually the toughest, and she goes through
several jobs before she gets the one she settles down in, if she
can be said to settle down. In between jobs, of course, she
has the most difficult time. The office is at first not a pleasant
place, but she gets to know it and can soon classify all its
people. There is the boss in the front, whose private
secretary she hopes some day to become. There are minor
executives and salesmen, who are eligible for marriage or
dates or at least good dinners. . . . Finally there is the old
man who is either a clerk or an accountant, and there are the
'fresh' office boys.

The love-story of the white-collar girl often involves
frustrating experiences with some boy-friend. When the

white-collar girl does not get her man, the experience hardens her, turns her from the simple, small-town girl to the cool, polished, and urbane career woman or bachelor girl. She has no objection to love affairs 'if she cares enough' about the fellow, but she cannot get over her interest in marriage.

After her first frustrating experience, however, love becomes secondary to her career. For she has begun to enjoy her position and is promoted; after the first level stretch she is always on the slight upgrade. As she becomes a successful career woman, her idea of getting an upper-class man increases, and she is too 'mature to interest the average male of her acquaintance'. Usually she prefers men who are older than she. After thirty, she looks back, somewhat maternally, upon the casual love life of the happy-go-lucky younger girls. Now she is a mature woman, efficient in her job, suppressing her love for her married boss, to whom she makes herself indispensable, doing the housework of his business. This relieves the impersonal business atmosphere and the tension between superior and employee.

from *White Collar* by C. WRIGHT MILLS

The author suggests two of the American girls' motives for taking up secretarial work. What are they? Are there other motives, perhaps?

Why do you think her first job is usually the toughest? How can a more experienced friend help the girl to adjust herself to her new job?

Are the problems the girl faces, as a newcomer, typical of all jobs?

Do you think that the picture presented in the last paragraph suggests that the 'successful career woman' is completely happy?

How far does the passage sound as though it is typical of what might happen in England? Is it true only in places? Is it not true at all?

Toads

'Toads' is a poem expressing some attitudes to work that most people experience at some time in their lives.

Why should I let the toad WORK
   Squat on my life?
Can't I use my wit as a pitchfork
   And drive the brute off?

Six days of the week it soils
   With its sickening poison—
Just for paying a few bills!
   That's out of proportion.

Lots of folk live on their wits:
   Lecturers, lispers,
Losels, loblolly-men, louts—
   They don't end up as paupers.

Lots of folk live up lanes
   With a fire in a bucket;
Eat windfalls and tinned sardines—
   They seem to like it.

Their nippers have got bare feet,
  Their unspeakable wives
Are skinny as whippets—and yet
  No one actually *starves*.

Ah, were I courageous enough
  To shout 'Stuff your pension!'
But I know, all too well, that's the stuff
  That dreams are made on:

For something sufficiently toad-like
  Squats in me too;
Its hunkers are heavy as hard luck
  And cold as snow.

And will never allow me to blarney
  My way to getting
The fame and the girl and the money
  All at one sitting.

I don't say, one bodies the other
  One's spiritual truth;
But I do say it's hard to lose either,
  When you have both.

by PHILIP LARKIN

What does the writer mean by saying work is a toad?

Do people work 'just for paying a few bills', as the writer suggests?

What have the men who live on their wits achieved?

Do you think the writer envies the people who 'live up lanes'?

Why does the poet want to shout 'Stuff your pensions'?

He has daydreams as we all do; what prevents him from fulfilling them?

The Mass Media

ADVERTISEMENTS

The language of advertising

Advertisers have brought the art of propaganda very near
to perfection. A consideration of the devices employed in
advertisements may help us to recognize the tricks of other
propagandists and to consider how immense and insidious is
their influence. The advertiser has something to sell; it
would be unreasonable to expect him to be disinterested. He
wishes to present his goods in the most favourable manner
possible. Accordingly he is unlikely to provide us with all the
information that would enable us to form an independent
opinion of the value of the article advertised. Frequently he
has to create in us a felt want for his goods. Accordingly he
will seek to arouse our emotions, appealing to our desire to
be healthier, or more beautiful, or better dressed than we
are. At the same time the skilful advertiser will support this
appeal with some show of evidence that his goods are able to
satisfy these desires.

Look at the advertisements in any newspaper or magazine
that is at hand. Following my own advice I select a few
specimens, slightly camouflaged to prevent complications.

A man and a girl gaze at each other. An inscription says
that as long as men can see they will respond to beauty.
Then follows the advice: 'Use this cream and awake the
response that she does.'

A patent medicine is offered as an infallible cure for a
common chest complaint. A promise is made that even the
most obstinate cases will yield to this treatment. There
follow 'letters of gratitude selected from hundreds'. A
woman writes that she despaired of ever being well, but
now she is 'a different woman'. Eminent medical men and
well-known public persons (unspecified) are said to have

51

praised the treatment. The reader is assured: 'Health is
your right.' He believes that he has been offered evidence
that this medicine will enable him to attain this right.

Notice how often you see advertisements containing such
captions as the following:

> They all swear by ——.
> Everybody is doing ——.
> We are going to do ——. Are you?
> Trust the —— baker.
> Trust your dentist. HE knows a good tooth-paste.
> Some who know GOOD —— made this.
> Goodbye to doubts when you see —— trademark.
> Send them happy to school. Give them ——.
> You want a healthy baby, don't you? Then ——.
> Here's value you never saw before. Why not get a
> ——?
> This is the brand that is used by men of action, men
> who DO things.
> *This* soap is different.

These captions, often accompanied by pictures, are
designed not only to arrest your attention, but also to appeal
to your desire to do as others do or to obtain something
which, it is suggested, would be good for you. Something is
wrong with you and the advertisement tells you to trust the
expert upon whom you must in the end rely. The advertiser
reckons upon your not pausing to ask for any evidence that
'they all' swear by the goods offered, nor for any evidence of
the credentials of the 'expert' who hides so modestly behind
the description. The purpose of the whole layout of the
advertisement is to persuade you that you have been
offered reliable evidence, although, in fact, you have not.

from *Thinking to Some Purpose* by SUSAN STEBBING

'The advertiser has something to sell; it would be unreasonable to expect him to be disinterested.' What does the writer
mean when she says this?

Why is the advertiser unlikely to provide us with all the information needed to form an independent opinion of the value of the article?

The writer says the advertiser has to create in us a feeling that we want his goods. Express in your own words how he manages to do this, according to the author.

In the advertisement by the patent medicine firm the advertiser assures us in three different ways that the medicine will meet our needs. What are the three assurances? Comment on any one of them.

Look carefully at the advertisement captions. Choose one and try to show how the advertiser is presenting his product and trying to persuade you to buy it.

Cough remedies

Most doctors will tell you that you would be foolish to try yourself to treat a SEVERE or PERSISTENT cough. No amount of the cough remedies we discuss in this report will cure a cough caused by serious infection or disease.

There are, however, many unpleasant but relatively mild illnesses, like those we call 'colds in the head' and 'laryngitis', which can cause an irritating cough and soreness of the throat. These usually get better quickly—if they do not, you should see your doctor—but, until you do recover, there are medicines and pastilles that claim to soothe the throat and ease the cough. The chemists' shops are full of them, and we must spend a great deal on them to justify the £1 million spent on advertisements for cough and cold remedies last winter. Are any of them any good?

There are over fifty proprietary preparations which are available direct to the customer. CA asked a chest specialist to comment on the sixteen brands of pastilles and seventeen brands of liquids which are among the most popular and most advertised. CA's consultant judged how effective each preparation was likely to be, by noting the amount of each ingredient in the dose recommended on the bottle. He has divided the remedies into four groups, basing his judgements on the ingredients whose action is known. The results are set out in the Table, together with CA's calculation of the cost of a dose of each of the preparations. No account was taken of the time for which each dose would be effective. (A TABLE FOLLOWS IN THE ORIGINAL.)

What is coughing? Coughing is the natural way of draining excess phlegm uphill through the mouth. This is beneficial and should not normally be prevented. 'Useless' coughs may be caused by irritation of throat or air passages. This can result from breathing in irritants like smoke or fog or from some minor infection of part of the respiratory passages. The act of coughing is a protective reflex, like blinking.

To relieve a cough caused by irritation, you can either try to SOOTHE the site of the irritation or take a drug which SUPPRESSES the cough by acting on the cough centre in the brain.

To help coughing to clear excess phlegm, drugs called EXPECTORANTS have been used for many years to make the phlegm less thick and sticky. More recently, to help people with coughs whose air passages are narrowed—as in asthma and some sorts of bronchitis—drugs called ANTI-SPASMODICS have been given. CA would not advise the constant use of antispasmodics without reference to your doctor.

None of the remedies we have discussed will *cure* your cough; they will act as *palliatives*. If you want simply to ease your cough and have the feeling you are doing something about it, CA suggests that a general purpose mixture with a reasonable dose of *suppressant* and *expectorant* is probably your best bet. If you simply want something to suck to soothe an irritation, we suggest that you have the pastille or sweet whose taste you find most agreeable.

Note. We have only discussed here *adult* cough mixtures. Some of the mixtures we have discussed, particularly those containing morphine and codeine as suppressants, are unsuitable for children.

adapted from *Which?* November 1960

The medicines examined in this report are often called 'cough remedies'. Is this a fair claim? Why do you think the article goes to some lengths to explain how a cough is caused?

Think of several advertisements for products that are supposed to cure us. How many of these give explanations of illness in similar detail to the C.A. report? Do you think they should?

What expert evidence is the chest specialist in the report called on to give?

Compare the evidence of the chest specialist in the report with the kind of comment made by unnamed doctors in popular advertisements. Do you notice any differences?

Re-read the report. Which important pieces of information are rarely or never found in advertisements? What conclusions do you draw?

Exact? Clear? Misleading? Exaggerated?

SINO clears nasal infection within hours. Sino, the modern scientific discovery, contains Hexogermaline and two other vital ingredients in a new capsule form. Thoroughly tested by experts, both scientifically and medically, it has relieved the suffering of tens of thousands.

Feeling feverish?—Here's the painkiller you've been looking for. Developed after years of dedicated research, *Sino* puts you on your feet again and helps you fight those feverish headaches and winter miseries.

R—C 83312c

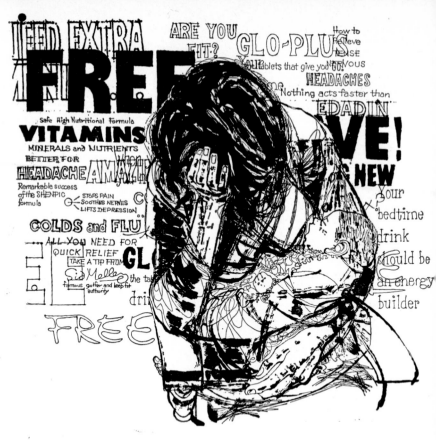

Don't wait for flu to attack! Kill it before it starts with a capsule every day. Sino leaves you better than healthy, for every capsule provides you with a double boost of daily vitamins. Ward off that 'winter gloom'.

More and more doctors are recommending *Sino*. Don't wait a day longer! Buy *Sino* now!

CINDEROCK: for driving dependability and peak performance when you need it most choose CINDEROCK. When you drive on CINDEROCK you drive with the assurance that you've obtained the ultimate in tyre safety and performance. CINDEROCK Rubber X, the exclusive new tread rubber available only in CINDEROCK tyres, provides extra protection against punctures, blowouts and skidding. This revolutionary tyre material, combined with the CIN-

DEROCK Safety-Fortified cord body, provides a totally new type of high-performance tyre.

New SMOOTHE clears unsightly teenage skin blemishes swiftly . . . quickly . . . reaches the root of infection, sinks right into your skin. It works invisibly—no one can see it on your face—checks infection and clears away blemishes quickly. SMOOTHE'S antiseptic ingredients include Hexachlorophene, the medically approved antiseptic that promotes rapid healing for most common skin troubles: spots, pimples, sunburn, bites and stings, minor cuts and burns. It's so pleasant to use too: non-greasy, non-staining, you just smooth it on your skin. You can feel how mild and kind it is. SMOOTHE—and see how quickly your skin troubles go!

Get into a NITSU and out of the ordinary! When Guiseppina designs a motor car he sets the fashion for years to come. It just stays at the top. And the NITSU is every inch a fashion-setter! This car is designed to pamper its driver in every out-of-the-ordinary way. When you drive it you feel it. Styling, finish, performance, petrol consumption—all are exceptional. So get into a NITSU and out of the ordinary. NITSU looks years ahead.

Look at any one advertisement.

Is there any evidence offered that this product is better than others?

What claims are made for the product and are they supported with evidence?

Pick out any five words or phrases which sound persuasive or impressive. Criticize one of them.

What effect did this advertisement have on you when you first read it?

Do you feel convinced that the product is worth buying? State your reasons for or against.

NEWSPAPERS

Control of the Press

An examination of our newspapers shows that the great
majority of them are extraordinarily uniform with regard
to what news is included, what omitted, and what comments are made. On those occasions when newspapers of
rival political views take up strongly opposed sides there is
very seldom any discussion of the views of the other side.
Few newspapers report the opinions of foreigners about
British policy, unless that opinion happens to be favourable.
There are honourable exceptions, but those newspapers are
not widely read. The lack of variety is not, on reflection,
surprising. I was at first surprised when I began to study
different newspapers. This was so because I had not reflected
upon the fact that most of the newspapers with the biggest
circulations are owned by a comparatively small group of
men. Sixteen London newspapers (ten daily papers and six
Sunday papers) are owned by five groups of proprietors.

These groups also own a large number of provincial newspapers. Papers belonging to one group naturally give the same news in much the same sort of way. The owners of these newspapers have an almost unlimited power to form the opinions of the reading public. 'Almost', but not quite, for the owners are themselves to some extent controlled by the big advertisers who are relied upon to provide the main revenue of the newspapers. The advertisers would not advertise in a newspaper that tended to undermine 'the confidence of the public'. The advertisers want the readers to be ready to spend their money; the newspapers want the advertisers to spend large sums in advertising their goods.

That the Press should be thus controlled constitutes a serious obstacle to our obtaining the information we require in order that we should think to some purpose about public transactions. I have used the word 'controlled' because, in the ordinary sense of the word 'free', our Press is remarkably free, notwithstanding the laws of sedition, blasphemy and libel. These laws affect the Press neither less nor more than they affect the private citizen. Books, pamphlets, journals, supplements to newspapers, can be and are in fact published which criticize and condemn the Government of the day in a manner that would not be tolerated in many countries. This we all know, and are apt to congratulate ourselves on. But here lies a peculiar danger for the majority of the readers. We tend to believe that we have a 'free' Press because we know it to be legally free. But the Press is in fact controlled by a comparatively small number of persons. The danger lies in the fact that the majority of people are not aware of the ownership. Consequently, when they see different newspapers providing the same news and expressing very similar opinions they are not aware that the news, and the evaluation of the news, are alike determined by a single group of persons, perhaps mainly by one man—a Press Lord.

from *Thinking to Some Purpose* by SUSAN STEBBING

The writer says that 'most of the newspapers with the biggest circulations are owned by a comparatively small group of men'. Two things follow from this. What are they?

In what way are newspapers to some extent controlled by advertisers?

Do you think there are dangers caused by newspapers depending so heavily on advertisers for their main source of revenue? Explain the reason for your answer.

The writer says that in some ways our Press is 'remarkably free'. What exactly does she mean by the word 'free'? What example does she give to prove that there is this freedom?

What are the dangers caused by the fact that the majority of people do not realize that the Press is controlled by a small number of Press Lords?

Extracts from the daily Press for 13 April 1961

GEORGE THE GREAT

THE WORLD WENT BLUE FOR EIGHTY NINE MINUTES

THE INTRIGUING QUESTION THEY ASKED Yuri GAGARIN today after he came back from his orbit of the earth was: What did it LOOK like? 'The sky is very, very, dark,' he said, 'and the earth is a light blue.'

And that is about as much as 27-year-old Gagarin would say about his epic journey.

It is a journey for which Moscow radio acclaims him 'The Columbus of Space', scientists declare 'the road to the planets is open', and dancing, celebrating crowds dub him Yuri Veliki, George the Great.

Gagarin (it means wild duck) was blasted off at 7.7 a.m., orbited over Africa and South America in 89·1 minutes, and landed in Western Russia at 8.55.

Grinning

He climbed out of his rocket capsule unaided, wearing a light blue space suit with pointed helmet, and fell with a huge grin into the arms of waiting pilots.

His cheeks were kissed, his hands were shaken, his back was slapped. He seized an old friend in a bear-hug and wrestled with him.

In a tense, chart-lined control room miles away the telephone rang. A man at the landing point reported: 'Yuri Gagarin is with us.' And soon the news was flashing round the world.

George the Great took a helicopter to head-quarters. The 'phone rang again. It was Krushchev.

'How are you—how was it?' the Soviet leader asked Gagarin. 'I am well,' he replied. 'I could see oceans, mountains, big cities, rivers and forests.'

Then: 'Tell me, Yuri, are you married?' Gagarin said: 'Yes, I have a wife, Valentina, and two daughters—Elena, who is two, and Galina, one month.'

Krushchev asked: 'And your wife—did she know you were going to fly in the cosmos?' Gagarin said: 'Yes, she knew.'

'Please give my sincere greetings to your wife and children,' said Krushchev. 'We shall celebrate this great exploit. Goodbye till we meet in Moscow soon.'

Relaxing

A few formal words: Major Yuri Gagarin, member of the Communist Party speaking. Then his fine, rugged face relaxed and he was young Yuri, a poor farmer's son who was trained as a moulder, fought his way to technical school, and became a full-time flier only four years ago.

Krushchev sent him a message: 'All the Soviet people will remember your flight for centuries to come.'

As Gagarin blazed that lonely path into space and fame, his 26-year-old doctor-wife was at their two-roomed flat near Moscow looking after the children.

The living-room, with model Sputnik and spacedog setting off the TV set, filled with friends tonight.

Valentina must have known about the projected flight about the time baby Galina was born. But she said simply: 'My husband left home several days ago, simply kissing me and the kids, saying he would be back soon.'

She added: 'Yuri is very fond of modern poetry and art. He is a great sportsman. I am terribly proud.'

Perhaps Gagarin's mother guessed too. As he took off she was praying in church. . . .

THE DAILY EXPRESS

WORLD ACCLAIM FOR SPACE EXPLORER

SOVIET HONOURS SHOWERED ON MAJOR GAGARIN

Moscow appearance expected tomorrow

At 07.07 (British Summer Time) yesterday the Soviet Union fired the first man into space. One hundred and eight minutes later, after circling the earth once, 27-year-old Major Yuri Alexeyevich Gagarin landed at 'a predetermined spot' in the Soviet Union. After the 'cosmonaut's' landing the Soviet Communist Party and Government issued a statement proclaiming Russia's lead in the space race and appealing for world peace and disarmament.

Moscow took on an excited May Day aspect. All Russia (says Reuter) went wild with joy over the epoch-making voyage of the man whom Moscow radio called the Columbus of the Interplanetary Age.

Major Gagarin will probably be in Moscow tomorrow to receive the plaudits of Moscow and the world.

He was already being showered with honours yesterday. He was awarded the title of 'Master of Radio Sport of the Soviet Union'. Russian statements, however, emphasized the collective nature of the space triumph and claimed it as a victory of the socialist system.

Krushchev Message

The first glowing message to the spaceman came from Mr Krushchev on holiday on the Black Sea. The message said:—

Dear Yuri Alexeyevich, it is a great joy to me to congratulate you heartily on the occasion of the outstanding heroic feat—the first cosmic flight in the Vostok (East) spaceship satellite. The entire Soviet people acclaims your valiant feat, which will be remembered down the centuries as an example of courage, gallantry and heroism in the name of service to mankind.

The flight made by you opens up a new page in the history of mankind in its conquest of space: it fills the hearts of Soviet people with great happiness and pride for their socialist motherland.

With my whole heart I congratulate you on your happy return to the homeland from your space journey. I embrace you. Until our meeting in Moscow soon.

Mr Krushchev later spoke by telephone to Gagarin. Tass said that Gagarin thanked him for his congratulations and then said: 'I am happy to report to you that the first space flight has been successfully completed.'

Just Like Home

Mr Krushchev told Gagarin that by his exploit he had made himself an 'immortal man'.

Mr Krushchev asked how Gagarin felt, and he replied: 'I felt well. All the equipment of the space ship worked accurately. During my flight I saw the earth from a great height. I could see seas, mountains, big cities, rivers, and forests.' He had felt well in the spaceship 'like at home'.

'I shall be glad to meet you in Moscow,' Mr Krushchev said. 'You and I together, with all our people, will solemnly celebrate this great exploit in the conquest of space. Let the

63

whole world look and see what our country is capable of, what our great people and Soviet science can do.'

Gagarin said: 'Let all countries now catch up with us.'

Mr Krushchev replied: 'You are right, let the capitalist countries catch up with our country, which has blazed the trail into space and sent up the first cosmonaut in the world.'

Mr Krushchev asked for his hearty greetings to be sent to Gagarin's wife and children and parents. He concluded, 'You have done a deed which will live through the centuries. Goodbye till our meeting in Moscow soon. I wish you all the best.'

THE TIMES

MY SPACE STORY

by the only living man who knows

Today the Daily Sketch salutes and congratulates spaceman Major Yuri Gagarin and the Russian scientists who achieved the Twentieth century dream of making him the first man to return alive from space. A world gasping with admiration will read his eye-witness report on the centre pages. But our wonder doesn't end there. We wonder too—

DID MOSCOW SWITCH DATES?

Was Yuri Gagarin actually in the sky from 7.07 a.m. until 8.55 a.m. yesterday while Moscow kept the world cliff hanging by the radio wondering if the hero would live to tell the tale?

Not a chance of it, say news analysts.

It is thought that Russia replayed the whole drama—a lie in the sky—several days after it actually happened.

Russia, say the experts, would never have put themselves in a position where they might have had to say: 'Sorry, we seem to have lost contact with Gaga.'

Anyway, it was all just a bit too pat.

These are the alternatives considered likely:

1. Gaga made his trip on Friday OR—

2. He did so in a stand by rocket after another astronaut, Gennady Mikailov, had been shot into space and run into trouble.

The White House said that American experts tracked something in space yesterday.

But that could have been an existing satellite or a new one—without a man aboard.

Mr There-and-back

He zooms round the world in just 5,346 seconds.

The fastest man alive, Major 'Gaga' Gagarin (his name means wild duck) landed his four-and-a-half ton spaceship with just a slight bump and told the world:

'The sky was very, very, dark and the earth was light blue. Everything was clearly visible.'

Mr Spaceman 1 had zoomed in orbit around the world in 89 min. 6 sec. And to overcome the pull of the earth's gravity his rocket ship reached speeds of 20,000 miles per hour.

This is how an on-the-spot-correspondent—Russia has not released the name of the landing base—described his first sight of 27-year-old Major Yuri Alexeyevich Gagarin:

'Stocky, smiling as only a truly happy man can, he was coming down the gangway of the aircraft.

'He was wearing light blue, sky colour overalls and a flying helmet.

'People struggle to embrace him, they congratulate him and kiss him.

'Gagarin hugged one of his friends. The mood was good and gay.

'His eyes shine as if the lights of the stars are still reflected in them.'

By one of those supreme ironies, the man who helped Russia achieve the most spectacular of scientific successes in man's history is a carpenter's son.

His first message back to earth came forty-one minutes after take-off.

From his hermetically sealed cabin about 150 miles above South America he said:

'Flight is proceeding normally. I feel well.'

THE DAILY SKETCH

Each newspaper gives a special slant to this important news.

Study each one and try to decide what general impression you get from each report.

Look carefully at the three headlines and try to decide how far they illustrate a difference of approach to reporting the story.

Look carefully at the way each newspaper names the cosmonaut. There are obvious differences. What is the distinctive appeal each has?

Two articles report the conversations between Mr Krushchev and Major Gagarin. What are the main differences in emphasis in the two reports? Can you explain these apparent differences and discrepancies in wordings? Can you also offer a suggestion why each newspaper reported the conversation in the way it did?

Two articles describe the cosmonaut's landing. In actual fact no English newspaper reporters saw this landing. The information was given to the world by the Soviet News Agency, Tass. Do the reports give this impression? Also do you notice any differences in detail, despite the fact that all newspapers received the same information?

Does any report seem to you to be more truthful than the others? If so why do you think it is?

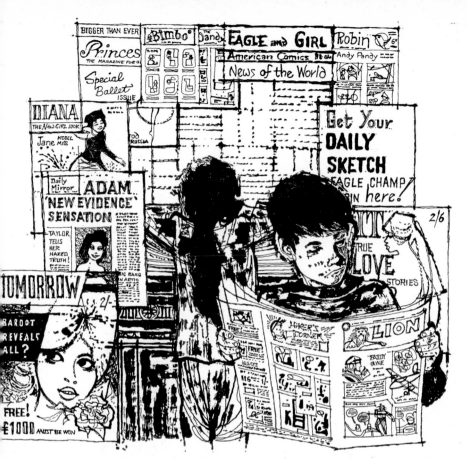

COMICS AND MAGAZINES

Boys' weeklies

The other thing that has emerged in the post-war boys' papers, though not to anything like the extent one would expect, is bully-worship and the cult of violence.

If one compares the *Gem* and *Magnet* with a genuinely modern paper, the thing that immediately strikes one is the absence of the leader-principle. There is no central dominating character: instead there are fifteen or twenty characters, all more or less on an equality, with whom readers of different types can identify. In the more modern papers this is not usually the case. Instead of identifying with a school-boy of more or less his own age, the reader of the *Skipper*, *Hotspur*, etc., is led to identify with a G-man, with a Foreign Legionary, with some variant of Tarzan, with an air ace, a master spy, an explorer, a pugilist—at any rate with some single all-powerful character who dominates everyone about him and whose usual method of solving any problem is a sock on the jaw. This character is intended as a superman, and as physical strength is the form of power that boys can best understand, he is usually a sort of human gorilla; in the Tarzan type of story he is sometimes actually a giant, eight or ten feet high. At the same time the scenes of violence in nearly all these stories are remarkably harmless and unconvincing. There is a great difference in the tone between even the most bloodthirsty English paper and the threepenny Yank Mags, *Fight Stories*, *Action Stories*, etc. (not strictly boys' papers, but largely read by boys). In the Yank Mags you get real blood-lust, really gory descriptions of the all-in, jump-on-his-testicles style of fighting, written in a jargon that has been perfected by people who brood endlessly on violence. A paper like *Fight Stories*, for instance, would have very little appeal except to sadists and masochists. You can see the comparative gentleness of the English civilization by the amateurish way in which prize-fighting is always described in the boys' weeklies. There is no specialized vocabulary. Look at these four extracts, two English, two American.

> (1) 'When the gong sounded, both men were breathing heavily and each had great red marks on his chest. Bill's chin was bleeding, and Ben had a cut over his right eye.
>   Into their corners they sank, but when the gong clanged again they were up swiftly, and they went like tigers at each other.' (*Rover*)
> (2) 'He walked in stolidly and smashed a club-like right to my face. Blood spattered and I went back on my heels, but surged in and ripped my right under his heart. Another right smashed full on Ben's already battered mouth, and,

68

spitting out the fragments of a tooth, he crashed a flailing left to my body.' (*Fight Stories*)

(3) 'It was amazing to watch the Black Panther at work. His muscles rippled and slid under his dark skin. There was all the power and grace of a giant cat in his swift and terrible onslaught.

He volleyed blows with a bewildering speed for so huge a fellow. In a moment Ben was simply blocking with his gloves as well as he could. Ben was really a past-master of defence. He had many fine victories behind him. But the Negro's rights and lefts crashed through openings that hardly any other fighter could have found.' (*Wizard*)

(4) 'Haymakers which packed the bludgeoning weight of forest monarchs crashing down under the axe hurled into the bodies of the two heavies as they swapped punches.' (*Fight Stories*)

Notice how much more knowledgeable the American extracts sound. They are written for devotees of the prize-ring, the others are not. Also, it ought to be emphasized that on its level the moral code of English boys' papers is a decent one. Crime and dishonesty are never held up to admiration, there is none of the cynicism and corruption of the American gangster story. The huge sale of the Yank Mags in England shows that there is a demand for that kind of thing, but very few English writers seem able to produce it. When hatred of Hitler became a major emotion in America, it was interesting to see how promptly 'anti-Fascism' was adapted to pornographic purposes by the editors of the Yank Mags. One magazine which I have in front of me is given up to a long, complete story, 'When Hell Came to America', in which the agents of a 'blood-maddened European dictator' are trying to conquer the U.S.A. with death-rays and invisible aeroplanes. There is the frankest appeal to sadism, scenes in which the Nazis tie bombs to women's backs and fling them off heights to watch them blow to pieces in mid-air, others in which they tie naked girls together by their hair and prod them with knives to make them dance, etc., etc. The editor comments solemnly on all this, and uses it as a plea for tightening up restrictions against immigrants.

On another page of the same paper: 'LIVES OF THE HOTCHA CHORUS GIRLS. Reveals all the intimate secrets and fascinating pastimes of the famous Broadway Hotcha girls. NOTHING IS OMITTED. Price 10c.' 'HOW TO LOVE. 10c.' 'FRENCH PHOTO RING. 25c.' 'NAUGHTY NUDIES TRANSFERS. From the outside of the glass you can see a beautiful girl, innocently dressed. Turn it around and look through the glass and oh! what a difference! Set of three transfers 25c.', etc. etc. etc. There is nothing at all like this in any English paper likely to be read by boys. But the process of Americanization is going on all the same. The American ideal, the 'he-man', the 'tough guy', the gorilla who puts everything right by socking everybody on the jaw, now figures in probably a majority of boys' papers. In one serial now running in the *Skipper* he is always portrayed ominously enough, swinging a truncheon.

This is an extract from an essay written by

GEORGE ORWELL in 1939

Orwell believes that the life of a superman is not as admirable as many think. Can you suggest why this might be so? Would you agree with him?

Think of the exploits of some supermen you have read about. Would you say that Orwell's comments apply to these supermen that you are familiar with?

What kind of character do you tend to identify yourself with as you read a story? Can you suggest why you do this?

Why should Orwell feel a dislike of the 'leader-principle' and the 'central dominating character' in boys' magazines?

Orwell says there is a difference between the English and American weeklies. Look at the four extracts. What differences do you see?

Orwell suggests that the magazine 'When Hell Came to America' is a bad one for boys. What reasons does he give for his opinion? Do you feel that the writers of such magazines are 'cashing in' on human suffering?

Spicy magazines

To return to the magazines themselves; there are a number of 'spicy', 'off-the-shoulder' periodicals, or sex-and-bittiness weeklies and monthlies, whose bark is in an illuminating way much worse than their bite. They can be bought from almost any newsagent, not only from the 'magazine shops', and some of them have considerable sales. I have not been able to find figures of their distributions by class, but know them to be popular among working-class and lower middle-class young men.

They are, first, repositories of jokes, many of them illustrated and with the emphasis on very obvious, limited and only moderately exceptionable sexual innuendoes. Each of them usually has a crossword, a page on sport, fortune-telling-by-the-stars, and short-short stories. The stories might be expected, from the layout and drawings, to be sexy, but prove to be as domestically whimsical as those in a modern women's home magazine. The narrator is a young man who is either not long married or, to judge from the mildness of his whistles after the girls, won't be long before he settles down with a decent lass.

Nowadays there is sometimes a film-serial, with décolleté photographic illustrations. For the rest, there are a great many drawings of various sizes, with jokes underneath. Most of these magazines aim to be very smart and modern, although in general their layout is hardly slicker than that of some family magazines. They establish their claim to modernity and sophistication largely by using artists in the newer style. Their pages have not, therefore, the quieter domestic lines of the older magazine artists, but rather those of the Englishmen who have learned from the Americans, notably from Varga. There have to be photographic pin-ups, and in the absence of a considerable use of colour photography and some of the more expensive devices which help their rivals, most of these magazines seem to try to ensure that their photographs shall be as daring as possible and that the models really shall appear to be coming right out of the page at the reader.

They are all consciously sexy-naughty, aware that they are being daring, having a bit of a fling, at least in their illustrations. But obviously one can feel like that only by assuming the existence of values which one is flouting. There is little that is ingrown or over-heated about these magazines; they belong to the same world as the older women's magazines, after all. The strongest objection is not to their sexiness but, as so often with the newer kinds of magazine, to their triviality: they get the thrill of naughtiness so easily and on such slight and spurious evidence.

from *The Uses of Literacy* by RICHARD HOGGART

The writer calls the magazines 'sex-and-bittiness weeklies and monthlies'. From what he says about them in paragraph 2, what exactly does this phrase mean?

What seems to be the main difference according to the writer between these magazines and the older family magazines?

Look carefully at these two sentences in the last paragraph: 'They are all sexy-naughty, aware that they are being daring, having a bit of a fling at least in their illustrations. But obviously one can feel like that only by assuming the existence of values which one is flouting.' What do you think the writer means in the second sentence? Do you know of any magazines like these—what do you think of them?

Now you have read the whole passage look back at paragraph 1. What do you think 'whose bark is in an illuminating way much worse than their bite' means?

72

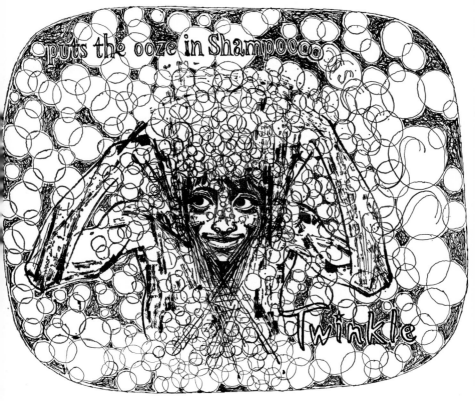

TELEVISION

Westerns

In every series seen the central character is a hero of quite outstanding qualities (the eleven-year-old Ken in 'Flicka' has all the potentials of the future hero). What do they share in common? A sense of justice, courage, physical and moral strength, confidence, intelligence and an exceptional portion of good looks. They are always ready to take up a just cause and have a strongly developed sense of duty to right wrongs. They are all unbelievably quick on the draw, can use their fists to good advantage and their horsemanship is impeccable. They are an abstract of good against evil.

There is a considerable variation in their ages, ranging from the youthful Brewster to the more mature Favor. All these heroes with one exception share one thing in common with the arch villains, they are never hampered by human attachments of a domestic nature. The exception is Tom in 'Laramie' who lives with, and cares for, two younger brothers. Their attitude to women is always chivalrous, they often inspire love on the part of the women, but rarely show more interest themselves than good manners require and a natural admiration for a young and pretty woman may prompt.

They are never the initiators of violence but in practically every case are involved in it up to the hilt by the end of the story. Shooting in self-defence or to save another's life is the hero's usual excuse for violence, more often than not preceded by one or more bouts of fisticuffs. In Cobb's case ('Whiplash') it is not the gun but the boomerang that gets his man but although he makes a parade of not using a gun because of setting a bad example, he uses a knife, a boomerang and a whip with as much relish and skill as is ever shown by the others with their guns.

As a fair generalization it can be said that, although they make little or no protest when violence is carried out on their behalf, they are, for the right reasons, reluctant to use it themselves and this applies particularly to Favor who, in the three examples of 'Rawhide', is never once himself personally involved in an act of violence. . . .

The standards and attitudes of the characters emerge in the above generalizations as, indeed, do the values which are conveyed through the story, but some are deserving of a more particular reference. Violence must take precedence in a discussion of Westerns as it is the stuff of which they are made, it is usually the pivot of the plot and nine times out of ten it serves as the final arbiter. A Western without it or its ever-present threat would be like an egg without salt. It is, therefore, not the fact of violence that needs discussing but the kind of violence, the amount, its rele-

74

vance to the plot and above all the way in which it is depicted.

Shootings and fist fights are present in all these films, in most cases in considerable quantity, more, indeed, than is strictly necessary to the plot. Apart from shooting and fist fights, other kinds of violence shown include the use of boiling acid to dispose of the villains, a knife fight, the use of a whip as a weapon, and refined torture by means of a hypodermic syringe, the threat of which is used to make the villain confess. On three occasions women are treated with sadistic brutality. Close-ups are, on the whole, used sparingly but the hypodermic syringe incident is filmed in close-up, the emotions of tormentor and tormented inescapably imprinting themselves on the viewer's mind. The visual impact of the fighting is often reinforced by the very noticeable sound of fist meeting flesh and bone.

Everyone knows that in the Wild West (as depicted in Westerns) justice is rough justice and the law, if it exists at all, is personified in a Marshal who is either a super hero or a crooked impostor. Of the latter we have no examples in our viewing but the hero marshal is epitomized in the character of Wyatt Earp. He fervently believes that a man is innocent until he is proved guilty and he is as much concerned to save the innocent man as to track down the guilty one. In most cases justice is done by the liquidation of the wrongdoers. In only one case, 'Flicka', is the situation resolved by the timely arrival of the police. In four instances the law does not figure in any guise and in the others, apart from Maverick who is nearly hanged on false information, the law steps in merely to pick the crusts.

from *Family Viewing*

by the COUNCIL FOR CHILDREN'S WELFARE

Look at the list of qualities that the Western heroes are said to share. Now draw up a list of qualities you consider essential for a real-life hero and compare the two lists. What differences do you notice?

75

The Western heroes are 'never hampered by human attachments of a domestic nature', says the report. What do you think it is getting at?

The report acknowledges that violence is a natural part of Western stories but suggests that sometimes it is overdone and used for its own sake. Do you agree?

In what ways is violence made sadistic? What effect could this have on an audience?

In the Wild West the only justice was rough justice. Rough justice may have been a virtue in that society; do you think there are any dangers if people apply it to our society?

The family's defence of television

Children and parents alike try to present television as a beneficial influence on the family. When children in the main survey were asked: 'What are the most important ways in which television has really changed things at home?' 21 per cent. of the older and 13 per cent. of the younger viewers singled out the fact that the family was at home more or that its members saw more of one another. As many as 18 per cent. and 20 per cent. respectively of these two age groups made the even more important point that viewing improved the general tone of things at home, that there was more to do and talk about, that the family got on better together, and that there was more 'peace and quiet'.

It is natural that both children and adults should point to television's good effects. The mothers who were interviewed showed a strong tendency to take up a defensive attitude about television, at least as far as their own family was concerned. The majority insisted that television made no difference to their family life and relationships, to conversation within the family, to their children's behaviour, or to their domestic routines. Asked about effects generally, they assumed these must be ill effects, and gave such answers as 'Oh, there are no effects on *our* children'; only sixteen out of the sixty mothers mentioned any bad effects— mainly confined to late nights and bedtime difficulties.

Several factors lie behind this defensiveness. First, much has been said and written about the possible bad effects of television, and it is understandable that parents should interpret 'effects' in an adverse way. It is equally understandable that they should be anxious to exempt their own children from undesirable reactions. It is also possible that parents wish to think of television more as a family bond than as a family menace, and that mothers in particular may see it unconsciously as a means of postponing their children's independence, and of cementing family unity. Parent viewers have a vested interest in presenting television as something of a benefactor, and as a result, especially in working-class families, it tends to be regarded in an uncritical manner.

Even fathers can be included in this rosy picture of television as a home-maker:

> 'Television hasn't changed us. Television holds you together. Before we had television, it was very difficult to keep my husband contented. My children have grown up that bit more, and their interests are inside now; when you have a fire it's very cosy. I only wish we'd had television sooner. They eat up more now because they sit and watch television and don't notice how much they eat . . . before they used to run away. Their interest doesn't end with the programme. I don't have much hope for Mary for the scholarship, but television wouldn't be the cause if she fails. There's more to converse about, with you having television. There's questions, and one thing leads to another. . . . Television doesn't command our life. It gives us a lot of pleasure— for people in our position, by the fire with the children. We haven't always got something to talk about. Television helps to create interest around the family fireside. After being demobbed it was very difficult to keep my husband

77

occupied. Television keeps husbands at home. Young men don't go to the pubs so much.'

For the working-class family especially, as in the example just quoted, television may in fact offer a common interest and conversational source such as had hardly existed previously. Television is also useful as a pacifier—it keeps husband and children quiet; sometimes it is almost thrust at children, especially when very young. One mother, for instance, found she could keep her baby quiet by holding it up to look at television.

Although most mothers denied that they used television as a means of discipline, incidental remarks made elsewhere in the interviews suggested that they sometimes did just this. For instance:

'My children behave rather better now that I have television. You can kind of bribe them with television. If they want to see a programme or a person, they'll behave.'

Roughly half the children in both age groups of our main survey sample said that their parents sometimes allowed them to view later as a reward for good behaviour; and 18 per cent. of the older children and 32 per cent. of the younger said that television was sometimes withheld as punishment.

from *Television and the Child* by HIMMELWEIT,
OPPENHEIM & VINCE

Would you say that a home with a television set had more 'peace and quiet' than a home without one?

Would you agree with the argument put forward by many mothers that television has made no difference to their family life and relationships?

Most mothers said that there were no effects on their children. Do you feel that television has had no effect, good or bad, on you?

The report says that television, especially in working-class families, tends to be regarded in an uncritical manner.

78

Would you say this was true of your family and your friends? For example, how often do you switch off a programme you think boring?

Do you agree with the statement 'There's more to converse about, with you having television'? Over the last week would you have found as many varied subjects to talk about if you hadn't had a set?

What do you think about the idea of bribing children with television?

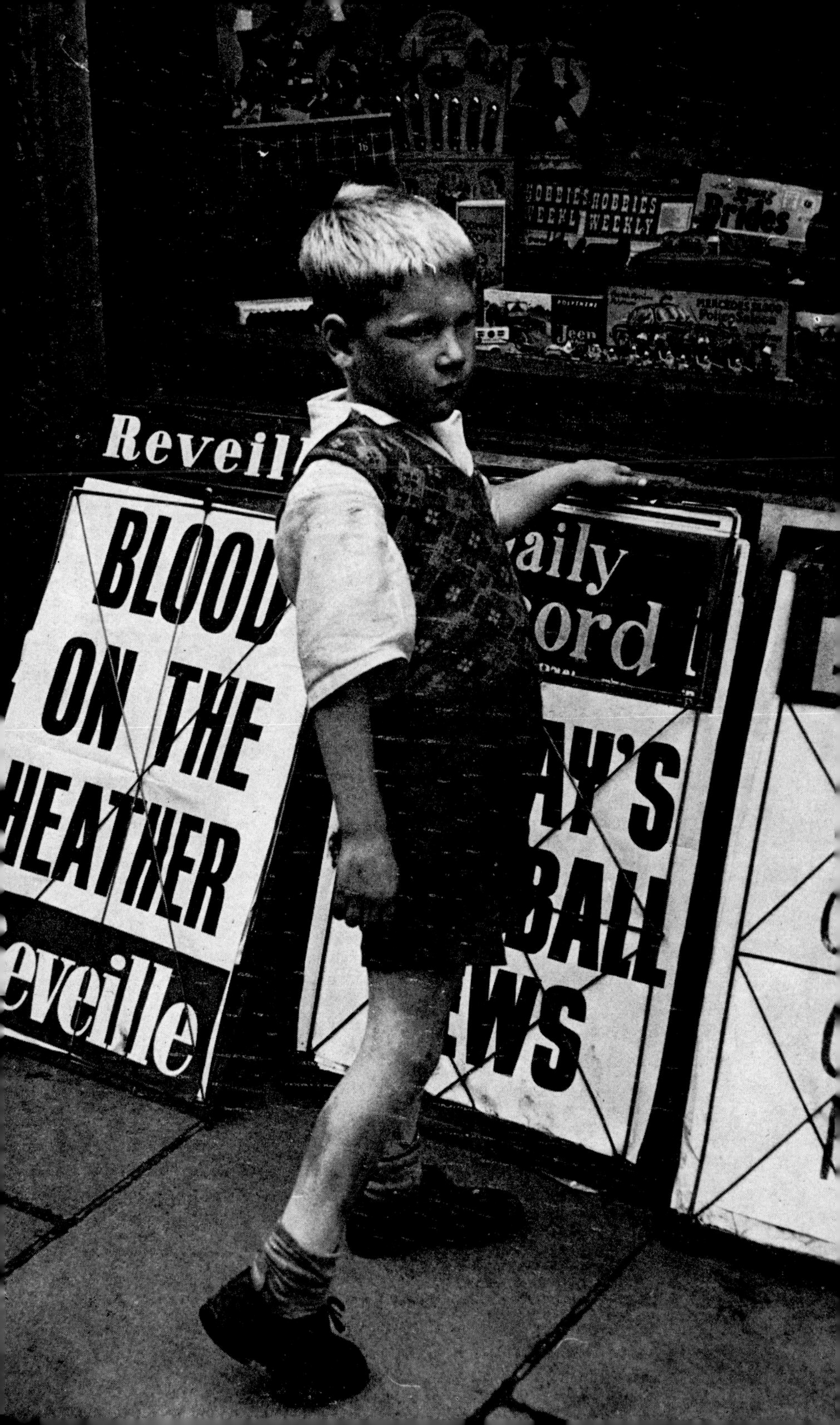
HOBBIES WEEKLY
HOBBIES WEEKLY
Brides
BLOOD
ON THE

BRITISH SHIPBUILDING LEADS THE WORLD

British Achievements Speak for Britain

Questions of Our Time

FREEDOM AND AUTHORITY

The pay packet

Arthur lives with his mother on Tyneside. He has recently
left school and just finished his first week at a new job. It is
Friday and after being out for the evening with a gang he
has returned home late.

I walked into a regular little scene of domestic bliss. . . .
The Old Lady was sat at one side and Harry at the other,
the radio playing softly, and you could see that they'd been
having the kind of natter that is possible only between
very good friends. It caught me on the raw.

'So you're in,' said the Old Lady, switching rapidly from
one tone to another. This is a talent I've noticed among the
ladies.

'Hello, all,' I said and sat down at my place, which was
set.

'His Lordship wants servin'.'

'Aw, Ma, let's have a meal in peace.'

'Look under your plate for your supper.'

'Ah, think Ah'll turn in now,' said Harry.

'Stop in and see the entertainment,' said the Old Lady.

'Yes, stay,' I said. 'Join in the fun—when we know what
it's all about.' But all the same I knew what it was all about
and also what lay under my plate.

'No thanks, Peg,' he said. 'Ah'll keep me nose out. . . .
Ah'm off.'

'Pity he didn't stay to hear ye sayin' your lines,' I remarked to his back.

'Now will ye shut your trap or ye'll have the teapot over
your head again,' said the Old Lady. 'Ye talk about me
goin' on—ye don't give anybody a chance to keep their

tempers and say a word in calmness.' Which, of course, was perfectly true. What is it that keeps you talking when you know it's no good? Especially to older folk. I've noticed they're slower to react—with words. They've the experience but the kids have the wit. But on you go stirring up the trouble. . . .

'Anyway,' I remarked. 'What's all the bawlin' about—it's a mystery to me, to date.'

'Ah'll give ye credit for more brains than that. . . .'

'Thanks,' I said.

'Ye know what it's about—your pay.'

'What's the matter—can't ye wait?'

'Ah told you that ye'd be on pocket money . . . then you deliberately go and break into your packet. What's the idea?'

'Let me ask ye a question: how d'ye know Ah've broken into it?'

'Well, look under your plate.' But I didn't: I wouldn't give her that pleasure. 'Look under your plate!'

'Ah don't need to look under me plate to know ye've been pokin' about in me room and rakin' about me private property.'

'And Ah don't think much about you,' she said. 'When Ah first started work Ah was proud to go home and hand me pay packet over to your grandma: proud.'

'Times have changed since then. . . .'

'For the worse. Ah'd burn with shame if Ah were you—after the way Ah've toiled and moiled to bring ye up—and on me own—ye turn round and do this.'

'Listen, Ma,' I said, trying to get things on to a reasonable plane. 'Just listen. *Ah'm* going out to work, not you. What was good enough for you doesn't hold for me . . . oh, it's all right, Ah'll pay me way; Ah'll give you board and lodgings. But Ah'll handle me own money. Ah'll buy me own clothes. Ah'm sick and tired of being taken and told what Ah'm to wear.'

'You'll hand your pay over—intact.'

'Ah'll pay you board and lodgings—that way we'll both be independent.'

'So's you can splash your money on your fancy monkey suits and keep up wi' your low friends, that's your idea. Well, Ah'm tellin' ye now: Ah'm not havin' it.'

Brushing the plate aside I took up the pay packet and extracted three pound notes: 'There you are. There's your money and be content.' I held them out but didn't get any reaction. So I slapped them bang in the middle of the table. 'All right—Ah'll leave it there an' you can pick it up when Ah've gone in your usual manner.'

'Ah'd burn before Ah'd touch it.'

'Pity you aren't so particular about other things.'

We were both on our feet now and ready to cut. 'What d'ye mean by that crack?'

'That fancy man of yours.'

'Why you little b——' It wasn't the teapot this time, but the breadboard. Well boy, I'm telling you, I didn't stand to attention. She was berserk, running wild, and coming for me. I ducked and came up and because I was frightened slapped her. She stopped dead. Then she turned and walked over to the chair in the corner and sat down.

'Ah'm sorry, Ma,' I said, following her.

She didn't say a word. She could have said: 'You struck me!' but didn't and I'm bound to admit I admire her for that touch. But I reckon I'd really hurt her. That slap had hit her right on the other solar plexus. 'Ah didn't mean it, Ma, it was just that you were comin' for me. But Ah didn't mean to hit you . . . like that.' By this time I was kneeling in front of her and she caught hold of my head and drew me to her. I reckon I was bubbling like a bairn.

'Ah'm sorry, Ma. Take the pay, all that's left. Ah shouldn't have done it.' Well, that's what I said, but I'm bound to admit that at the same time I was thinking myself a mug for giving in so easily. And then I was ashamed. 'No, lad,' she said. 'Ah don't want your money. God knows Ah don't want it. Ah just want to put things right between us, and Ah can't, and it gets me mad. Keep the money but be all right with me.'

from *The Day of the Sardine* by SID CHAPLIN

What makes the boy resist his mother's demands?

Do you feel he puts his case well? For instance, what do you notice about his attitude towards her?

How far do you feel the mother's demands are reasonable or right?

Can you suggest any likely reasons why they are reacting in this way to each other? Have you met anything like this in your own experience?

86

If they could have solved their problems any other way, what would they have needed to consider?

CREATIVE WRITING

Think of some of the turning points in your own life, incidents that have changed your feelings and attitudes to your parents or a teacher or a friend. Make a mental list of them if you like. They needn't be as violent as the one Sid Chaplin has created here. But each one is a key to your own growth and development.

As you look back, which incidents do you want to write about? Do they show something of the conflict that you read about above? Take one of them and write about it, choosing your own style, manner and method. Try to look beyond the incident: look to see how it might express freedom and authority in your own life, and your reactions to both of them. Look to see how you yourself were feeling and perhaps changing. Can you even show what the experience was like for both sides?

When you really mean and feel what you write, then you write well.

The arrest

At midnight Rubashov, a high party official, wakes from his recurrent dream of being arrested and hears hammering on the door.

The two men who had come to arrest Rubashov stood outside on the dark landing and consulted each other. The porter Vassilij, who had shown them the way upstairs, stood in the open lift doorway and panted with fear. He was a thin old man; above the torn collar of the military overcoat he had thrown over his nightshirt appeared a broad red scar which gave him a scrofulous look. . . .

It was cold, dark and very quiet in the staircase. The

younger of the two men from the Commissariat of the Interior proposed to shoot the lock of the door to pieces. Vassilij leant against the lift door; he had not had the time to put on his boots properly, and his hands trembled so much that he could not tie the laces. The elder of the two men was against shooting; the arrest had to be carried out discreetly. They both blew on their stiff hands and began again to hammer against the door; the younger banged on it with the butt of his revolver. A few floors below them a woman screamed in a piercing voice. 'Tell her to shut up,' said the young man to Vassilij. 'Be quiet,' shouted Vassilij. 'Here is Authority.' The woman became quiet at once. The young man changed over to belabouring the door with his boots. The noise filled the whole staircase; at last the door fell open.

The three of them stood by Rubashov's bed, the young man with his pistol in his hand, the old man holding himself stiffly as though standing to attention; Vassilij stood a few steps behind them, leaning against the wall. Rubashov was still drying the sweat from the back of his head; he looked at them short-sightedly with sleepy eyes. 'Citizen Rubashov . . . we arrest you in the name of the law,' said the young man. Rubashov felt for his glasses under the pillow and propped himself up a bit. Now that he had his glasses on, his eyes had the expression which Vassilij and the elder official knew from old photographs and colour prints. The elder official stood more stiffly to attention; the young one, who had grown up under new heroes, went a step closer to the bed; all three saw that he was about to say or do something brutal to hide his awkwardness.

'Put that gun away, comrade,' said Rubashov to him. 'What do you want with me anyhow?'

'You hear you are arrested,' said the boy. 'Put your clothes on and don't make a fuss.'

'Have you got a warrant?' asked Rubashov.

The elder official pulled a paper out of his pocket, passed it to Rubashov and stood again to attention.

88

Rubashov read it attentively. 'Well, good,' he said. 'One never is any the wiser from those things; the devil take you.'

'Put your clothes on and hurry up,' said the boy. One saw that his brutality was no longer put on, but was natural to him. A fine generation have we produced, thought Rubashov. He recalled the propaganda posters on which youth was always represented with a laughing face. He felt very tired. 'Pass me my dressing-gown, instead of fumbling about with your revolver,' he said to the boy. The boy reddened but remained silent. The elder official passed the dressing-gown to Rubashov. . . . They watched him as he got slowly out of bed and collected his crumpled clothes together.

The house was silent after the one shrill woman's cry, but they had the feeling that all the inhabitants were awake in their beds, holding their breath.

Then they heard someone in an upper storey pull the plug and the water rushing down evenly through the pipes.

from *Darkness at Noon* by ARTHUR KOESTLER

How do people in the house react to these policemen?

What differences do you notice between the two men who come to arrest Rubashov?

Can you suggest any reasons why the younger man behaves as he does?

Look at Rubashov's comment on the warrant. What does this suggest about the system of justice?

Imagine someone in your neighbourhood being arrested in the middle of the night. How do you think the policeman or the neighbours might behave?

CREATIVE WRITING

This is another violent scene, an abuse of authority. None of us have really been in this position, but some of us have been in situations rather like it: an arrest; being confronted by a tough, bullying gang; being caught doing something wrong. Think of how you feel, the thoughts that go through your mind at such moments; are you frightened by the absence of authority or do you want to resort to an authority of force, a sort of rough justice? What might all this lead to?

Choose whether you want to describe such an experience, or to put down your ideas on the justice and injustice that you personally have observed—or to do both these things.

A lynching

Horace Benbow is a lawyer who has unsuccessfully defended a crook wrongfully accused of murder. It is the evening following the conclusion of the trial. Horace is staying in a hotel near the jail where the convicted man is being held.

He heard the clock strike twelve. Then—it might have been thirty minutes or maybe longer than that—he heard someone pass under the window, running. The runner's feet sounded louder than a horse, echoing across the empty square, the peaceful hours given to sleeping. It was not a sound Horace heard now; it was something in the air which the sound of the running feet died into.

When he went down the corridor towards the stairs he did not know he was running until he heard beyond a door a voice say, 'Fire! it's a . . .' Then he had passed it. 'I scared him,' Horace said. 'He's just from Saint Louis, maybe, and he's not used to this.' He ran out of the hotel, on to the street. Ahead of him the proprietor had just run, ludicrous; a broad man with his trousers clutched before him and his braces dangling beneath his nightshirt, a tousled fringe of hair standing wildly about his bald head; three other men passed the hotel running. They appeared to come from nowhere, to emerge in midstride out of

nothingness, fully dressed in the middle of the street,
running.

'It's a fire,' Horace said. He could see the glare; against
it the jail loomed in stark and savage silhouette.

'It's in that vacant lot,' the proprietor said, clutching his
trousers. 'I can't go because there ain't anybody on the
desk. . . .'

Horace ran. Ahead of him he saw other figures running,
turning into the alley beside the jail; then he heard the
sound of the fire; the furious sound of gasoline. He turned
into the alley. He could see the blaze, in the centre of a

vacant lot where on market days wagons were tethered. Against the flames black figures showed, antic; he could hear panting shouts; through a fleeting gap he saw a man turn and run, a mass of flames, still carrying a five-gallon coal-oil can which exploded with a rocket-like glare while he carried it, running.

He ran into the throng, into the circle which had formed about a blazing mass in the middle of the lot. From one side of the circle came the screams of the man about whom the coal oil had exploded, but from the central mass of fire there came no sound at all. It was now indistinguishable, the flames whirling in long and thunderous plumes from a white-hot mass out of which there defined themselves faintly the ends of a few posts and planks. Horace ran among them; they were holding him, but he did not know it; they were talking, but he could not hear the voices.

'It's his lawyer.'

'Here's the man that defended him. That tried to get him clear.'

'Put him in, too. There's enough left to burn a lawyer.'

'Do to the lawyer what we did to him. What he did to her.'

Horace couldn't hear them. He couldn't hear the man who got burned screaming. He couldn't hear the fire, though it still swirled upward unabated, as though it were living upon itself, and soundless: a voice of fury like in a dream, roaring silently out of a peaceful void.

from *Sanctuary* by WILLIAM FAULKNER

Imagine the scene at the beginning of this extract. What effect has the sound of running feet on Horace?

What further is suggested when three men 'emerge in midstride out of nothingness'?

Look at the picture Horace sees as he turns into the alley. How does it strike you?

What impression do you get of the crowd?

Horace, the lawyer, is an innocent man. What do you think of the suggestion that he should be treated in the same way as the prisoner he defended?

What does the last line 'a voice of fury like in a dream roaring silently out of a peaceful void' suggest to you?

CREATIVE WRITING

In *Sanctuary* the writer is working out something through his own feelings, finding out what real anarchy might be.

Through your own imagination try to see your area in a state of total disorder. This is not so impossible: there is often some place in the world experiencing it.

What about those great masses and crowds you have been with at football matches: supposing they had got out of hand? Perhaps you have been in a crush . . . in rush hour . . .?

What about a dream you have had when you have felt powerless among strange forces you couldn't understand?

You may give this experience a better chance to come to the surface if you write a poem, not a story.

*   *   *

Have you ever been in authority?—looked after younger children, helped to run a dance or a game, worked on a committee perhaps. What does it feel like? What problems does it raise? Maybe other people treated you differently as a result. Try to express some of this experience. Conversely, what is it like when you suddenly want to be free and abandoned, feel a sudden impulse to go wild, to throw off all restrictions and get away from convention and authority?

When have you found authority at its most reassuring and helpful? When has it seemed at its worst? Can people protest against bad authority—without creating anarchy? These and many similar questions are worth thinking over, investigating if you like, and deciding about. How balanced can you be in putting down what you have observed and in drawing conclusions?

CRIME

Causes of crime?

In 1954 over 725,000 people were found guilty by the criminal courts in England and Wales. What happens to them after their conviction is clearly a matter of vital im-

portance to society. It is not only the offenders themselves who are affected. Crime is a serious burden on the community. The cost of the police, of the courts, of the penal institutions, is heavy. But society suffers in other ways, not measurable in pounds, shillings and pence, when some of its members go counter to the accepted pattern of its civilization and prey on their fellow citizens, instead of co-operating with them to the common good. The question how far, and in what way, the penal system can contribute towards the reduction of crime is therefore a matter of general concern.
. . .

*   *   *

A distinguished criminologist is discussing some probable causes of crime. After considering the importance of poverty, bad housing, unemployment and other material conditions, she now looks at more personal factors.

Another group of causes of vital importance centres round the home and the condition of life in early childhood. . . .

The influence of the moral standards of the home is self-evident. If there is no recognition of the difference between right and wrong, no value placed on self-control, on consideration for others or on the acceptance of responsibility, it is hard for the child to acquire the qualities necessary for good citizenship. Unwise discipline is another, almost equally obvious, factor frequently found in the background of the young offender. It may be unduly harsh or arbitrary on the one hand, or over-indulgent on the other, or it may oscillate between the two extremes . . . so that the child is alternately spoilt or clouted. . . .

But important as these two factors are, they do not cover the whole field. The practical experience of those who work with juvenile delinquents has demonstrated how greatly behaviour is influenced by the emotional relationships that exist within the family circle, whilst modern psychology, searching more deeply into the springs of action in both

95

adults and children, has given a new profundity and intensity to this point of view. The extent to which there is affection between the parents and the child, and in the early stages especially between the mother and the child, is of fundamental importance to his development. Lack of love is far more likely to produce delinquency than bad material conditions. . . .

Moreover, it is through the giving and receiving of love in those vital early years that a child's powers of affection grow. Like his muscles, they cannot develop if he cannot exercise them. If he grows up without experiencing affection in the home, he may become unable to give out any warm affection at all. He will never learn to consider the interests or well-being of other people, since consideration is not compatible with indifference. Unless he is fortunate enough to come into contact with someone who can give him what he should have got from his parents, he is likely as an adult to show the callousness which is typical of so many offenders. . . .

Children who are quite incapable of affection are, however, less common in the juvenile courts than those whose lack of feeling is in reality a form of self-defence. On the surface they appear to be entirely tough and callous. Underneath they are longing for an affection which has been denied them. It may be because the child is illegitimate or a step-child or was simply unwanted, but for one reason or another he has been ignored, or actively disliked, whilst perhaps affection has been lavished on his brothers or sisters. The realization of his neglect by someone he longs to please ultimately becomes so unbearable that he may consciously adopt a 'don't-care' attitude, but the pose becomes more and more set until it becomes part of the pattern of his life. . . .

We have stressed this matter of the child deprived of the warmth that should have nourished the emotional life of his early years, because this type of situation will be found described again and again in the case histories of adolescent

and adult, as well as of juvenile offenders. But there is the obverse side of the picture. The child who is spoilt and over-protected, who remains, even after childhood has passed, over-dependent on the mother, cannot develop into a self-reliant co-operative member of the community. He too may become delinquent because he cannot face the normal difficulties of life, but his delinquency will follow a different pattern from that of the deprived child. . . .

It is probable that in some respects adult criminals will never have grown out of their childish attitudes. . . . They may reach chronological manhood still keeping the self-regarding viewpoint of the nursery. They are unable, therefore, to cope with the demands of a highly complex society with its many taboos and its insistence on a type of behaviour based on very different standards from those of childhood. They still expect to snatch or hit back as the mood takes them, and society cannot tolerate this. Crime can in fact be regarded as essentially an expression of im-maturity, a continuation into adult life of modes of feeling and patterns of behaviour that are characteristic of a childish stage of development.

from *The English Penal System* by WINIFRED ELKIN

Make a note of the four qualities that the writer thinks necessary for good citizenship.

Why is it that the children of harsh or indulgent parents might well fail to develop these qualities?

What is suggested as the main reason why so many delin-quents show callousness? Do you think the explanation is convincing?

What feelings may be going on inside a child who puts on a tough appearance? Do you agree that this tough pose may become ingrained?

What might turn a spoilt or over-protected child into a delinquent?

In what ways are delinquents more childish than other people?

Courage of his convictions

In this extract a hardened criminal speaks for himself; he says frankly what he thinks about himself and his world.

What made me a criminal? . . . I could reel off a whole lot of reasons, but they'd all only be part of the real answer. I'm afraid of saying circumstances made me what I am, because I don't think they did entirely at all. Seeing my father, a straight man, getting only poverty all through his life for being straight, . . . living in an environment where nearly everyone I knew was dishonest, where stealing was a necessity at some times, an adventure at others, but was always acceptable whatever the reason . . . wanting to impress other kids, getting a reputation for being a tearaway . . . seeing the terrifying dreariness of the lives of other people who were 'straight' . . . not being able to face the idea of working for a living because I hated the idea of work. . . .

These were the circumstances, but they were only part of the answer. I still think I'd have been a criminal, whatever they'd been. For one thing there's this tremendous hatred of authority that I've got, this compulsion, almost, to defy it. I was born with that, I'm sure. Or I could say it was because I'd always had a desire for adventure, for living dangerously. That was true when I was young, but it isn't now, and I still go on. Now crime's just business, that's all.

When I came out of prison (after the war) the time for my discharge had gone by, and at least I was out of the Army. We parted from each other with mutual contempt. I'd half a mind to stay in Germany because there was a good living to be made with all the rackets going on. But the people who'd been home told me things were really rocking in London with all the shortages and black-market demand. I decided to go back and get in on it.

Going straight? I never even gave it a thought.

98

Right away in London I got into business, chiefly on buying and selling petrol and clothing coupons. It was easy, and the only thing wrong was I had to depend on other people for supplies, which were erratic and unsatisfactory: not business-like, in fact. So I started getting my own, breaking into offices, shops, garages, with a bit of ordinary screwing on the side.

Large blocks of flats in areas where wealthy people lived, like Knightsbridge and Chelsea for instance, paid very well. I rather fancied myself as a bit of an acrobat, and used to work from a rope fastened up on the roof, letting myself down outside until I came to a suitable window. There were always plenty of watches and jewellery lying about, and I soon learned how to value them before offering to a fence.

One evening I was in a flat when the woman who lived there came home. She started screaming for help, so I had to belt her. I'm not keen on using violence on women, but there's no choice if they start making a row.

It dawned on me after a bit that instead of picking up odds and ends it'd be quicker and more profitable to start further back along the line. I got up a firm with one or two reliable thieves, and we went into what might be called the wholesale side, knocking off any marketable commodity: cigarettes, groceries, cloth . . . I was learning all the time. . . .

Work was steady, living was comfortable, and I got myself a flat near Victoria and a car. My income level was on average well over a hundred a week.

But all good things come to an end. One Easter Sunday morning I was captured up on the roof of some flats in Highgate, and taken up to the Sessions in front of Fulton who was known as the 'Pontoon King'. He lived up to his reputation and I got twenty-one months, which I did in the Scrubs. It was dead easy compared with the army prison.

When I came out my old friend Pancho was at the gate to meet me. He took me over to Croydon where some friends of his called Paul and Ken lived. . . . They were working themselves at the wage-snatch business, with a bit of smash-and-grab on the side, and took me into their firm. We got on steadily for several months without any trouble. The living was much more reliable than screwing, where you were taking a chance on what you were going to get. . . .

One night we were doing a West End jeweller's, and the police whizzed round the corner the moment the hook went through the glass. Somebody'd tipped them. There was a bit of a punch-up, but they were ready for that, too. Pancho wasn't with us, so he was all right: but Paul and Ken got three years each, and I got two.

I did it in Wandsworth, and lost a bit of remission for fighting. When I came out Pancho got me in with another smash-and-grab outfit who took me on a job the very first night in Hendon. . . .

Time went on till I was captured again. . . .

I got took in after a few months for G.B.H. (Grievous Bodily Harm). . . .

Then I was captured trying to break a safe. . . .

Then I got three years for pussy hoisting (stealing furs) from a warehouse. . . .

Does any form of punishment have an effect *on me*? No, that's obvious, surely, isn't it? I can take punishment—in a way I can almost accept it as justified. The only thing that ever worries me is kindness; that gets under my skin a bit sometimes, it perturbs me. I haven't had a lot of it, so perhaps it's because I'm not used to it, but it does worry me all the same. Can I say this again here, though—that I'm not making a plea for more kindness in dealing with criminals. It's quite immaterial to me what method you try—but I think it's probably better for you, it does you less harm, to be kind.

from *The Courage of his Convictions* by
R. ALLERTON AND T. PARKER

What impression of normal life did Allerton form as he grew up?

Of all the reasons he mentions for his becoming a criminal, does any particular one seem more influential than the others?

Look at this man's actions and the tone in which he describes them. What characteristics besides courage has he got?

What seem to be the attractions a life of crime has for this man? Do you think a 'straight life' could possibly have the same attractions?

What is this man's attitude to punishment and serving prison sentences? Do you find this attitude surprising?

What suggestions would you make about the best treatment for a hardened criminal like him? Do you see any solutions?

101

CREATIVE WRITING

The *Courage of his Convictions* and Elkin passages begin to reveal the general problems facing man in dealing with people who have committed serious crimes. The difficulties are enormous and complex. Try to sort out your own ideas by writing them down. For instance, what activities going on in your area might easily lead to crime? What reasons— in your experience—have prompted the petty offences against other people that we see and hear about daily? How would you deal with young and first offenders, and how would you help prisoners ready for discharge? Think carefully about the implications of your ideas. Have you ever met and mixed with people convicted of crime? Imagine a prisoner returning home: what is he feeling? How is he affected by the people he meets and works with? Try to express these things.

Borstal boy

> At the age of 16 Brendan Behan was sent by the Irish Republican Army to commit sabotage in England. He was quickly arrested and sent to jail. Here he is being put into his cell for the first time.

I stepped inside and he slammed the door behind me, rose the cover over the little spy-hole in the door, and looked at me again, and re-locked it, and went off down the stairs on padded shoes.

I looked round me. I could walk five paces down from the door to under the window, which was too high in the wall, even if there was anything better than Liverpool to be seen or heard over the wall. There was a table and a chair, and a mirror, and a chamber-pot, and some bedboards, a mattress, and blankets. The floor was made of slate, and there

102

were also the rules to be read. I decided they were better than nothing, and when I had the bed made on the boards, it was alright. I got in between the sheets, and, though it was only a few inches off the floor, when I took up the rules and started to read them, I felt as comfortable as ever I did in my life. I was dead tired after that plank thing, or hand-carved couch in Dale Street, and was drowsy and falling off to sleep when I heard the cover of the spy-hole being moved.

'You all right, there?'

'Smashing, mate,' said I in gratitude.

'What do you mean, "mate",' said the voice from the door; 'where the bloody 'ell do you think you are— "*mate*",' he spat, vicious and indignant; 'and what do you think you're on, putting those notices on the floor, eh?'

'I was only having a read of them, sir,' said I, sitting up anxiously in my comfortable bed.

'Read them where they're supposed to be read, on the wall, not on the floor. Come on, get up and put them back.'

'Yes, sir,' said I, got up quickly, in my shirt, hung the rules back on the wall, slipped quickly back into bed, lay there breathing quietly till the screw dropped the cover of my spy-hole and went on to the next cell.

I lay in the dark, and heard sounds of outside, dim and mournful, away over the walls in the distance. A church bell rang out on the frosty air, and I got further down into the warm bed. Eight o'clock, it rang out. I'd have thought it was later than that, much later. It seemed like a year since I came from the court, but the bed was warm and comfortable after the bath, and I was tired after that Dale Street, and I was soon asleep, and half-eating the sleep till I got so far down into it I was unconscious. . . .

I was opened up again from my cell and brought down to the hall of the wing where we sat on our chairs in silent rows, about sixty of us, sewing mailbags. The class instruc-tor, they called the screw who went round showing the prisoners how to do the bags, and examined them or complained about the bad work when it was more or less than four stitches to the inch. That seemed to be the important thing, and most necessary for salvation.

He came over to me and sat down on a chair beside me and showed me how to wax the thread and put it through the canvas with the palm, which was a leather band with a thimble in the middle to save the skin of the palms, though sometimes even the most expert had to shove the needle through the canvas with their forefingers and thumbs, which in most of the prisoners were scarred like hands or arms of drug addicts with the needle marks you read about.

On Saturday afternoon we were locked up from twelve-thirty. The screw gave us a half-hour's exercise from twelve o'clock and remarked that it was handier than taking us out for exercise after dinner. It got the whole lot finished earlier, he said, and we could be left in our cells till morning. We all nodded our heads, and quickly, in agreement with him. It seemed the right thing to want to be locked up in your cell over the weekend, and I even felt my own head nodding when the screw said it was better to get the exercise over with so that we would not have to be opened up again after dinner.

So locked up we were, and Charlie and I and Ginger smiled at each other, so that the others would not know that we were not used to being locked in a cell from half past twelve on Saturday morning till slop-out at seven Sunday morning, and in we went. The dinner was old potatoes, cold, and a slice of bully beef and a piece of bread. This was always the Saturday dinner and I heard a screw saying that it was like that to give the cook a chance to get off, and after all he wanted a rest, too, and when he said that we all nodded our heads, and were glad the screw was so nice and civil as to say it to us.

from *Borstal Boy* by BRENDAN BEHAN

Think over the impression that this cell might have on an offender entering prison for the first time. What effect is it likely to have after a prisoner has spent some time in it?

Are you surprised at the way the warder speaks to Behan? Would you have spoken any differently?

Look at Behan's description of lying in bed in the dark. Imagine how you would have felt in the exact circumstances he mentions.

As their work, the prisoners were given mailbags to sew. What is the purpose of this work? Is there any alternative?

Read the passage again looking at all the details. What long-term effects would you expect this kind of prison to have on different sorts of people?

CREATIVE WRITING

How near have your own experiences been to a criminal's? How could you express the feelings of guilt, or the fear at some moment when you felt hunted? What is the nearest you have come to crime? You may know of people who have been mixed up with street gangs, or in trouble with the police. These questions may seem strange to you, yet we nearly all have these experiences and in writing about them it is surprising how much you learn about them, about yourself even, which you did not know before. Often that's why people do write: it helps them to see themselves.

These are personal matters. But at least if you write honestly about what you feel, and write with conviction, people can respect your work; they can only learn from reading it.

WAR

A visit to Peckham

Sir Winston Churchill recalls an incident in 1940 during the heavy German bombing raids on London when he was Prime Minister.

One day after luncheon the Chancellor of the Exchequer, Kingsley Wood, came to see me on business at No. 10, and we heard a very heavy explosion take place across the river in South London. I took him to see what had happened. The bomb had fallen in Peckham. It was a very big one— probably a land-mine. It had completely destroyed or gutted twenty or thirty small three-storey houses and cleared a considerable open space in this very poor district. Already little pathetic Union Jacks had been stuck up amid the ruins. When my car was recognized the people came running from all quarters, and a crowd of more than a thousand was soon gathered. All these folk were in a high state of enthusiasm. They crowded around us, cheering and manifesting every sign of lively affection, wanting to touch and stroke my clothes. One would have thought I had brought them some fine substantial benefit which would improve their lot in life. I was completely undermined and wept. Ismay, who was with me, records that he heard an old woman say: 'You see, he really cares. He's crying.' They were tears not of sorrow but of wonder and admiration. 'But see, look here,' they said, and drew me to the centre of the ruins. There was an enormous crater, perhaps forty yards across and twenty feet deep. Cocked up at an angle on the very edge was an Anderson shelter, and we were greeted at its twisted doorway by a youngish man, his wife, and three children, quite unharmed but obviously shell-jarred. They had been there at the moment of the explosion. They could give no account of their experiences. But there they were, and proud of it. Their neighbours regarded them as enviable curiosities. When we got back into the car a harsher mood swept over this haggard crowd. 'Give it 'em back,' they cried, and 'Let *them* have it too.' I undertook forthwith to see that their wishes were carried out; and this promise was certainly kept. The debt was repaid tenfold, twentyfold, in the frightful routine bombardment of German cities, which grew in intensity as our air-power developed, as the bombs became far heavier and the explosives more powerful. Certainly the enemy got it all back in good measure, pressed down and running over. Alas for poor humanity!

from *The Second World War* vol. ii

by SIR WINSTON CHURCHILL

Look at how the people react when Churchill arrives. Why do you think they reacted like this? What might have been their feelings?

What was there to fill him with wonder and admiration?

The young man and his family were proud of their experience. Do you think there was anything to be proud of? Would you have felt the same?

What is the mood of the crowd as Churchill moves off? Are their feelings understandable?

Churchill promises revenge but ends by saying 'Alas for poor humanity'. Can you explain this contradiction?

Counter-attack

Siegfried Sassoon fought in the trenches during the 1914–18
war. This poem is based on his experiences.

. . . A yawning soldier knelt against the bank,
Staring across the morning blear with fog;
He wondered when the Allemands would get busy;
And then, of course, they started with five-nines
Traversing, sure as fate, and never a dud.
Mute in the clamour of shells he watched them burst
Spouting dark earth and wire with gusts from hell,
While posturing giants dissolved in drifts of smoke.
He crouched and flinched dizzy with galloping fear,
Sick for escape,—loathing the strangled horror
And butchered, frantic gesture of the dead.

       *   *   *

An officer came blundering down the trench:
'Stand-to and man the fire-step!' On he went . . .
Gasping and bawling, 'Fire-step . . . counter-attack!'
   Then the haze lifted. Bombing on the right
   Down the old sap: machine-guns on the left;
   And stumbling figures looming out in front.
   'O Christ, they're coming at us!' Bullets spat,
And he remembered his rifle . . . rapid fire . . .
And started blazing wildly . . . then a bang
Crumpled and spun him sideways, knocked him out
To grunt and wriggle: none heeded him; he choked
And fought the flapping veils of smothering gloom,
Lost in a blurred confusion of yells and groans . . .
Down, and down, and down, he sank and drowned,
Bleeding to death. The counter-attack had failed.

from *Collected Poems* by SIEGFRIED SASSOON

How is the soldier feeling as he looks from his trench into the morning fog?

What happens to him as the bombardment gets under way? Do you believe that many men would feel like this?

The attack begins. What impression do you get of the fighting?

What impression do you get of death in war?

Is there anything in this poem that echoes Churchill's comment 'Alas for poor humanity'?

CREATIVE WRITING

We hope that on this topic you will never have to write from real experience. But just remember that many of your parents and grandparents suffered in the last great war, and even today, somewhere in the world, people are experiencing the horrors of fighting and bloodshed. Imagine what it is really like to be caught as children in an air raid: what are their thoughts and fears? Can you build up a picture of such a scene from their point of view?

Sometimes the films show a very glamorous and heroic picture of war, and boys long to read any number of stories about prisoners escaping. It seems so exciting and so safe when you are following the story at home. But what is it really like to be sitting in a trench, waiting; or what are the real feelings and fears of prisoners? Or imagine a casualty station or a refugee camp hurriedly set up: can you convey the experience of arriving there alone?

Hiroshima

On Monday, 6th August, 1945, the first atom bomb was dropped. The target was Hiroshima, a Japanese city; 60,000 men, women and children were killed and 100,000 injured. Kazuo, a fourteen-year-old boy, had just been forced to leave school and take up war work.

Kazuo was torn from this life among words and drawings when the Japanese warlords, in a last and already hopeless effort, mobilized the adolescents and drafted them to work in the munition factories. He was sent to the book-keeping department of the Mitsubishi shipyards, about one hour's travel by tram from his parents' home.

Even at this distance, in the suburb of Furue, miles from the centre of the explosion, the gigantic force of the blast had been felt and within seconds had turned everything topsy-turvy that stood in its way. Never would Kazuo forget the flash of piercing light, which might have been reflected from the flat of some enormous, polished, naked sword, nor the dull reverberation far away, *Do . . . doo . . .* which as it drew close was transformed into a sharp, painful and finally screeching *Ju . . . inn* that seemed to pierce through his ear-drums, and which culminated in a sound like a thousand thunderclaps, *Gwann!*, that hurled him into a bottomless abyss. From this derives the Japanese word *Pikadon*, for *pika* means lightning and *don* thunder. Then, like an apparition in a dream, he had seen the paper-white face of Miss Sakata.

She was hurrying as usual, a businesslike little figure who had just emerged from the boss's office, an account-sheet in her hand, and was coming through the door into the big room where the clerks worked. She suddenly stopped, her expression turning to one of annoyance as if irritated by the scene of deplorable disorder that met her eyes: the white pieces of paper whirling across the room, the telephones jolted from their cradles, the trickles of black and red Indian ink. She seemed to be on the point of turning on her heels when, with a scream of pain she could no longer control, her twisted body fell quickly forwards: a great splinter of glass, shaped like a fishtail, had pierced her back and now pinned her to the ground; it continued to vibrate, with a curious, high and extraordinarily delicate note.

The speed with which the pool of blood spread about her; the way her hands turned blue; the senseless running hither and thither of the other secretaries, with their black hair flying loose and their normally spotless white blouses stained with blood and filth; the helpless expression on the face of the chief clerk.

'Kacho-san, you must help her! Do something. Or she'll die.' Forgetting all the rules of politeness, Kazuo had shouted this at his superior: but this man, usually so filled with energy, had simply leaned motionless against his overturned desk. He could not grasp what had happened. He did not even try to stem the flow of blood trickling down his own face from the deep wound in his forehead.

The youth was still quite numb, but apparently uninjured. He jumped up and tried to draw out the cruel glass stiletto. He cut his hands and he could no longer grip it. So he wrapped a piece of cloth about the glass, that continued to vibrate, and tugged at it with all his strength.

The glass broke in his cut hands. At least a third of it remained in the wound. Miss Sakata's mauve lips opened and closed like gills as she gasped for breath. Then a tremor passed through her body, accompanied by a rattling sound. She was dead.

For many years Kazuo M. dared not summon up the memory of the horrors through which he had had to live on his way from the Mitsubishi Works through the panic-filled city. He had somehow managed at last to reach the quarter below Hijiyama Hill, where he lived. He had made it on foot and in his arms he was carrying the naked corpse of Sumiko, a girl with whom he had been to school. Mortally wounded, she had attached herself to him at some point during his passage through hell. Now he found the strength somehow to burn and bury her body. And somehow he survived the days that followed. His parents, too, and his younger sister Hideko had also been almost miraculously spared. They ate cold rice, pressed into balls and distributed by emergency mobile canteens. They slept in what had been an air-raid shelter, an unlit hole in the ground. This was a time of absent-minded handshakes, of wanderings as through a maze. Hair fell out, there was nausea and shivering fevers. And the most important thing was not to think deeply about the wounds being inflicted by the unspeakable events all about. To sleep, to sleep, to sleep! . . .

There are deserts of sand, deserts of stone, deserts of ice. But since August 1945, Hiroshima—or more exactly the spot where Hiroshima once stood—has constituted a new, peculiar and original sort of wilderness: an atomic desert, the handiwork of *homo sapiens*, and beneath its grey-black surface there still remain the traces of his activity and the pitiful remnants of his fellow-men.

The survivors, and the tens of thousands who lived elsewhere who had come to dig among the ruins for relatives and friends, gradually moved outwards in their search, away from the inner 'Circle of Death' until they were digging one, two and even three miles away from the point of maximum destruction. And the Circle of Death, this evil, harrowed, desolate expanse, now lay lifeless, enclosed within the green waters of the many-mouthed River Ohta, upon whose surface, with each ebb and flow of the tide, corpses, like autumn leaves, floated now upstream, now down: strangely enough the male corpses all floated upon their backs, the female ones upon their bellies.

Only a handful of foolhardy men now ventured into this no-man's-land. They dug in the ruins, searching for any buried object that might be sold for money.

It was in little groups of three or four people that they thus searched for loot, and they soon acquired a remarkable knowledge of the terrain.

. . . Towards the end of August 1945, Kazuo M. noted in his diary: 'Many rumours current in Hiroshima. For example, that the bomb contained poison. Anybody who breathed any of this in must die within one month. All grass and flowers will wither away.'

These rumours were almost universally believed, because many survivors who had been only slightly wounded by the *Pikadon*, or in many cases had not been hurt at all, became invalids on or about 20th August. Some of these rapidly developed the symptoms of what is today called 'radiation sickness' (when the whole body has been subjected to a massive dose of radioactivity), and died. . . .

The M. family also began to show the painful symptoms that revealed the radiation sickness. Setsuo M. complained that his eyesight had suddenly deteriorated, his wife began to lose her hair, while little Hideko vomited several times a day. Kazuo sat for hours each day in front of the entrance that led down to the air-raid shelter and stared out over the vast field of rubble. Later he attempted to recapture his mood as it had then been, in a poem that he sent me:

> It rains and rains,
> In the slanting rain I sit,
> It drums upon my naked skull,
> It drips across my singed eyebrows,
> It runs into that bleeding hole, my mouth.
>
> Rain on my wounded shoulders,
> Rain in my lacerated heart,
> Rain, rain, rain,
> Wherefore do I live on?

Doctors practising in Hiroshima at that time have recorded that a second phase now set in, after the first period of desperate and confused activity that followed immediately upon the *Pikadon*; many survivors now gave an impression of utter apathy and showed no wish to go on living. This symptom they called *Muyoku-ganbo*, and when they noted in a very sick patient's face an expression of listlessness increasing with each passing day, then they knew that there was no longer any hope of saving this particular life.

An eye-witness, the poetess Yoko Ohta, has described this

condition: 'Each of us had for a time done everything possible, without knowing for sure what exactly it was that we were doing. Then we awoke, and now we wished to speak no more. Even the sheepdogs that roamed about ceased to bark. The trees, the plants, all that lived seemed numb, without movement or colour. Hiroshima did not somehow resemble a city destroyed by war, but rather a fragment of a world that was ending. Mankind had destroyed itself, and the survivors now felt as though they were suicides who had failed. Thus the "expression of wanting nothing more" came to be seen upon our faces.'

from *Children of the Ashes* by ROBERT JUNGK

The office in which Kazuo was working was miles from the centre of the explosion. Compare the effects of the atom bomb with those of the large land-mine at Peckham.

Look at the scene in the office and the boy's walk through 'the panic-filled city'. What impression of the whole city do these two scenes suggest?

Within a few days thousands of people had come into 'the Circle of Death' searching for relatives and friends. Imagine yourself among them. Describe what you would have seen.

After about fourteen days Kazuo and his family begin to suffer violent after-effects. Look at these. What does this suggest to you about such bombs?

Read Kazuo's poem. What feelings seem to be expressed? Is what he says borne out by the comments on other survivors made by the doctors and Yoko Ohta?

Compare the Hiroshima survivors with those at Peckham. What differences do you notice and can you account for these?

When you think back over the whole passage, do you notice any groups of people who act quite differently from all the rest? Can you account for the attitude of these people?

The damage to cities, and the after-effects on people, that

are shown here were caused by one atom bomb. What power has a modern nuclear bomb? What do you think would be the effect of twenty such bombs on any country?

CREATIVE WRITING

Sometimes we feel that war must be prevented whatever the cost and the sacrifice. At other times we hear people say that war is inevitable. It's the same with armaments: some people feel we cannot be secure without nuclear weapons, others believe that while we possess nuclear weapons we cannot expect lasting peace. It is very difficult to decide who is the wisest; certainly a good deal of reading, thinking and cool discussion is necessary. When you feel you know enough about the precise dangers of modern war and the intentions of military planning, try to work out your own conclusions. Having to write them down on your own often helps.

R—E 833125

CO-OPERATION
AND PROGRESS

Adventure playground

Mr H. Turner was the warden of an adventure playground
in a poor district of London. Many teenagers used the playground as a club and Mr Turner decided to build with their
help a club workshop. They have just completed the building
only to be told by a government official that it does not con-
form to Ministry building specifications and will have to
be pulled down.

The next day, Phil and Malcolm came for a conference.
After we had demolished could we rebuild? 'If you think it's
worth it,' said Malcolm with his usual calm, 'then let's get

on with it.' Phil disagreed. 'It's supposed to be the boys' project,' he said. 'There's not much point in going on with it if they've packed up.'

The Masher was keeping a sceptical eye on our deliberations. None of the other senior boys had appeared. A couple of fathers waylaid me with a spate of questions and hints but could not offer any practical help. They had commitments.

The campers, however, had rallied round. Jock, Jerry and the twins had taken down the roof and were now stacking the sections behind the hut.

The next day, Phil and Malcolm came for a conference. 'Well, we'll help you get it down,' said Phil, 'and then we can talk about whether it's worth rebuilding. That's up to the boys; and I see none of them have turned up tonight.'

'Give them time,' said Malcolm. I was grateful for his understanding. I was still reeling from the blow, uncertain what we ought to do and doubtful what we *could* do. The prospect of starting all over again was appalling. Yet I was dismayed by Phil's attitude—'If they don't want it, then they'd far better do without it.'

The next evening we started demolition, helped by the campers Jock, Jerry and the twins. I have never felt so depressed, and the sight of The Masher eyeing us sceptically from a distance, added to my discomfort.

Then the tide turned. Ray had joined The Masher on the sidelines, the usual wet cigarette stuck on his lower lip and his small head jutting from his duffle collar in the usual tortoise-like attitude. They did not appear to be speaking but suddenly they reached a joint decision. The Masher, shouting encouragement and orders to the younger boys, plunged into the work. Ray nodded gravely at me, took his coat to my office and came back rolling up his sleeves.

When someone takes a lead, the others always seem to hear of it at once. Within a few minutes, Sandy and Nick had joined us and the evening ended, very late, in a changed atmosphere. Everyone had shown a great will to work, and over a final cup of tea I realized that a great deal had been

117

achieved, over and above the concrete results. The question of whether to rebuild was already out of date. We were only concerned with the details of how to set about it.

This time, we had the advice of a qualified architect, a good friend to the playground who gave us practical hints as well as professional plans. We felt a new confidence in what we were doing and I noticed a new spirit of steady enthusiasm. Progress was swift, in spite of difficulties. There was no money for concrete, no money for asbestos roofing. But the Chairman took her usual positive attitude. 'It's needed. So we'll find the money somehow.'

At this point, our builders' gang was presented with a problem they could not solve for themselves. The asbestos roof was too heavy for the supports. But there was no question now of giving up the struggle or passing the buck. They produced a friend of their own age, Stan, who was apprenticed to a joiner. Stan was a quiet and capable boy who sized up the situation in a thoroughly professional manner. In a couple of afternoons he had measured, cut and bolted the new supports, and the roof was safely fixed.

When at long last the building was completed, the boys held their first meeting in their own workshop to form their own committee.

from *Something Extraordinary* by H. S. TURNER

Look at the different ways people react to the calamity. Was this to be expected? How would you have felt?

The leader felt powerless to rally the boys, but the situation changed once The Masher started working. Can you explain what has happened?

The question of whether to rebuild was quickly forgotten. What carries the group through once they have restarted building?

At one stage the boys seem to be depending less on their leader. What do you feel they have learnt?—what sort of leadership is this?

The boys get help from several people. Do you think they could have managed on their own? Do you know of any projects where a group have succeeded without calling in outside help?

'If they don't want it, then they'd far better do without it' is Phil's attitude. People take this attitude in many situations. What mistake(s) are they making?

CREATIVE WRITING

Most of us are unconscious of the amount of co-operation that naturally takes place in our daily lives (we tend to notice the conflicts more easily!). Spend part of the day observing the ways in which people co-operate, at school, in the playground, the dining hall, the street, the bus or train, and at home. The results may be worth reporting.

On special occasions, though, we actually notice co-operation taking place. Has anyone been ill recently in your street?—it may be interesting to tell how neighbours reacted. Or again you may not have constructed a workshop, but there are many other team jobs you may have taken part in. Try to describe the most interesting and weigh up what different people got out of it.

Dolci: ideals in action

A young man, Danilo Dolci, had a very promising career ahead of him as an architect. Instead of pursuing this, he decided to go to a village in Sicily where many people lived in poverty. Two fishermen from the village tell the story of what he did.

One fine day on the one o'clock train Danilo came to Trappeto with 30 lire in his pocket. . . . You could see from his face that he was the son of Dolci who had worked here on the railway ten years back. . . .

119

Everyone there came up to him and asked him what he had come to do. He answered that he wanted to help them live as brothers. He said he had come to Trappeto to chuck in his lot with the poor.

After a bit when he had seen well and truly how things stood he said that one or two houses had to be made, as many as one could, and take the worst off in the village—orphans with no mother or father—and make sure that the little ones had food and clothing. . . .

Next morning he came with us and chose this spot called Serro. . . .

The next day we went to the owner of the ground to ask how much he wanted, and we made a price of 370,000 lire (£200). We told him that we had no money and he in good faith said we could start work. . . .

After a time he often came and talked with people in the village and they told him of their needs especially medicines that they couldn't get and as soon as he saw such a case he went at once to a doctor for a prescription and went to Balustrate to buy the medicine. . . .

Most of us in the village kept looking at him and asking how such a clever man could be at Trappeto, leading such a miserable life, amidst us poor people. He was even poorer than us who had nothing.

And when Danilo sees children in the street with snotty noses, he takes his handkerchief, bends down, blows their noses and gives them a kiss.

People questioned him as to what he wanted to do and he patiently told us what he was doing. He told us that the Lord wanted the world to live as brothers such as it is not doing now. . . .

Because if all were brothers these bad things would not happen—wars, people who kill, people who steal, unemployment, children dying of hunger, and people throwing things around because they have nothing to do.

The Lord does not want such bad things. Danilo wants to form a community where you live as everyone's brother.

120

People did not understand very much but little by little they learned.

One man from Trappeto said that when lamps were sent to Trappeto for night fishing, at first they sent the catalogue and you read it but you did not know how to light the lamp.

But after you had the lamp in your hands you soon learnt how to light it.

Then a man said to Danilo that just by reading the scriptures nothing comes out of it and you are not brothers but you have got to live the scriptures to understand them.

Next Sunday, men, women, children, the mayor and the priest of Balustrate as well went up the hill to see Danilo's land, the hut and him. And everyone was happy and asked him what he wanted to do. Danilo told everything and the mayor said that he would certainly help where he could.

Next day Danilo made an arrangement with the master-builder to build a house and the master agreed to work although there was no money, waiting until Providence sent it—'When it rains'. A man from Alcamo and another from Balustrate gave us mortar—without paying; that is to say these people had such admiration for Danilo and seeing that it was a sincere thing, a holy thing, they had faith in him.

Next day he went to Mazzara del Vallo to buy two wagon loads of bricks and had them sent cash on delivery hoping that when these wagons arrived, Providence would have sent the money.

As there was no money to pay for the bricks the wagons stayed for two days, costing 4,000 lire a day (£2). At last some friend lent him the money. And so he continued for all the rest.

As soon as the bricks arrived at the village we started building, Danilo first, pick in hand, with two others. He also loaded himself up with sand and gravel and carried it up the hill. There was a lane which the mules and horses carrying the sand could not pass through, and the others had to carry it up there on their shoulders. Danilo worked there for a

121

month or a month and a half, and as soon as the roof was put on the house he went and slept inside. As soon as the house was finished he went and bought furniture at Palermo, also without paying—'When it rains'.

At about the same time he started going to the public works office where Giuseppe Alessi gave a little money. With this Danilo paid a few debts. One day the credit notes for the furniture expired and the men who had sold it to Danilo came from Palermo in a terrible rage and wanted to take it away.

Then Danilo tried to convince them with good words but they were more enraged than ever, and shook him by the shoulder and threatened him that if he did not give over the money at once they would smash in his head.

But Danilo did not move and they called him a rogue and a cheat. The women inside the house were all afraid that they would take him to the police station at Partinico to charge him.

But Danilo kept calm and said, 'Because the father and mother of these children have died must they die? If you want my motor-bike in exchange take it. I have no money.' And they took the motor-bike with them to Palermo. After four months Danilo brought them the money and they gave him back the bike.

After the furniture, Danilo bought the bath and the lavatories, and this is the first house with a bath in it and all the people of Trappeto were amazed to see it. As soon as the house was finished we went to Balustrate to make a registered company of the house and land, and since it was necessary to give it a name, Danilo called it Borgo di Dio.

Meanwhile Danilo went around the place speaking with people and seeing what misery there was; and he began to think what he could do to help these people.

One day a man in handcuffs came from the railway with two country guards. He was being taken to Balustrate, because he had stolen a basket of grapes weighing perhaps four kilos from the property of a Trappeto man. He had been driven by hunger and had five children at home without food and his wife made the sixth. The youngest child of four months was sick. When Danilo saw the condition of that father who had stolen a few grapes to feed his children, he begged the two guards to let him go. But they went on taking him to the station at Balustrate.

Meanwhile the Trappeto men took pity on the father and went to Balustrate to beg the guards to let him go, and they did so.

Next day Danilo called this father to work with him because he felt some remorse and almost blame for not having taken him before, although the man had asked him for work so often, and he could not give it to him as there was none and no money to pay him.

At Borgo di Dio they said, 'Before he goes in gaol, we will go.' But having work, he did not go to steal any more and there was no fear that he would go to gaol.

Afterwards Danilo took care of this man and his family, and gave them pasta and bread, even though he had debts with the grocers.

Meanwhile in the village the men were looking for work and asked Danilo, 'Why don't you help us and give us work?' They asked him because he seemed to be the only person who could help us.

He tried to get money from the council at Palermo to open a small road-mending works for the unemployed at Trappeto.

Danilo saw that there was hope but it would take time and during this time someone would die of hunger. Twenty days after the house was finished he plucked up courage and without money took some men up to mend the road going to Borgo di Dio.

In the beginning there were about twenty men and when they came to work he told them, 'If you want to work stay with me. There is no money. When Providence sends it I will give it to you.'

The grocers gave the workmen food. They hoped Danilo would pay one day.

After a few days there were no longer twenty but forty and eighty men a day who wanted to work; and there was hardly room to swing a pick. This was all because there was no work and they were satisfied to work and wait for the money to arrive to pay the grocer. . . .

Meanwhile the work on the road was coming to an end and Danilo did not know what to do to help the poor in the village.

Danilo had realized that the River Iato was running into the sea and wasting its water. The water of this river could give the whole village work and even outside the village if it irrigated the dry land. . . . Danilo with the rest of us held a meeting.

At the meeting we said that there was no more work for men and in a little while there would be other children dying of hunger.

Then we wrote a letter to the council saying that it was necessary to provide at once the minimum help to remove extreme poverty from the village. We did not want help in family assistance but we wanted help to get the water from the river and spread it over the country.

If these things were not done at once, seeing the children were dying of hunger, Danilo would not eat any more.

Then we friends who were there said, 'Danilo first and us after', meaning that as soon as he died one of us would take his place.

from *Sicilian Documents* told by a fisherman

Why do you think Dolci felt it was essential to live with the poor villagers he wanted to help?

After Dolci has heard the story of the lamps, someone says, 'You have to live the scriptures to understand them.' What is he getting at and how does it link up with what Dolci is doing?

Dolci had no money, yet he managed to build a house for the orphans. What seem to be the reasons for his success?

Some of the people to whom Dolci owes money become violent. Can you explain how it is that he manages to handle them?

Look at all that Dolci does and feels in the episode where the man steals the grapes. What strikes you about his response?

Dolci takes some men to mend the road to the house. He tells them he cannot pay them, yet soon eighty men are working with him. Can you suggest why so many men came to work and what his object was in organizing this?

When unemployment and starvation in the village seemed inevitable, Dolci threatened to starve himself. Why do you feel he chose this form of protest rather than any other?

CREATIVE WRITING

Imagine some of the feelings Dolci must have experienced when he came as a stranger to this out-of-the-way village. What do you think made him stay? (Perhaps you can get some clues from the stories in his book *To Feed the Hungry*.) Try to express the feelings and thoughts of such a person, perhaps as he is looking at his life and wondering about his aims.

World poverty

The plight of the underdeveloped world is once again forcing its attention on the leading western industrial nations. After years of giving aid to Asia, Africa and South America it is slowly being realized that far from the gap between the 'haves' and 'have-nots' being narrowed, it is still widening. It was recently estimated that in the middle 1950s the average income per head of the 1,250 million people living in 100 underdeveloped countries outside the communist block was about $100 a year. This compared with $550 in the Soviet Union, $700 in the Common Market countries, $875 in the Efta countries (other than Portugal), and no less than $2,075 in the United States. The gap was big enough then. It is unlikely to narrow in future. Real income per head of population in the developed countries is rising at an annual rate of $2\frac{1}{2}$ per cent., compared with one of only 1 per cent. in the underdeveloped countries. Rich and poor throughout the world are moving still farther apart. What should be done about it?

The Times, 7 August 1962

The widening East-West gap

One of the most striking features of our contemporary world is the very uneven distribution of material wealth. Leaving aside the countries in the Soviet orbit, we have at the one extreme the highly industrialized countries of Europe and of North America and Australasia, with in round figures, a population of 400 million, and an average income a head of £300 a year (at 1949 prices).

In marked contrast to the rich west are the still pre-industrial countries, particularly those of Asia, Africa and South America. These—excluding Soviet China—have a population of some 1,000 million people and an average income of about £20 a year a head, that is one-tenth that of Europe and a still smaller fraction of that of the West as a whole. Moreover, this low income does not on the average seem to have increased much during the last three centuries and may at times have fallen, despite the revolutionary improvements in world technology as a whole during this period. It seems from such figures that 300 years ago the standard of life in at least the most advanced nations of the East, such as China, India or Persia, must have been as high as that of Europe. The gap now of ten to one in favour of Europe is of quite recent origin and is due to the sudden

126

advance of the West, mainly in the last 200 years, whereas the Eastern countries have remained nearly static.

Economists have recently been turning their attention to the complex historic causes which lead a country to transform itself from a static pre-industrial state to a growing industrial one. Making apt use of an aeronautical metaphor, the American economist Rostow has named this vital period of transition 'the take-off into sustained growth'. In Britain, the first country to become industrialized, this critical period seems to have been the last twenty years of the eighteenth century.

In the typical pre-industrial country, three-quarters or more of the population may be engaged in agriculture, and wealth tends to remain constant or rises but slowly. Savings and gross investment are low, some 5 per cent. or less of the national income, that is, only about enough to maintain a static economy by paying for the depreciation of existing wealth. After take-off, savings and gross investment rise till some 15 per cent. of the national income is available for gross investment, leaving around 10 per cent. for net new productive investment, On the average in the West today such new investment results in a rise of gross income of about 3 per cent. a year. . . . The fraction of the population engaged in agriculture steadily falls as social development and industrialization proceed, and agriculture itself becomes partly industrialized and so much more efficient. In Britain, the savings and investments required for the take-off were essentially provided by the prosperous classes who did not spend their surplus wealth on ostentatious living but invested it in productive industry.

Everyone recognizes that most scientific and technological innovations can lead to continually increasing wealth only when they became embodied in material things, particularly production goods such as machine tools, chemical and fertilizer plants, transport and communication systems.

In addition to maintaining its existing wealth, the Western world is saving and investing productively some

127

10 per cent. of its income of £300 a year a head; that is, some £30 a year a head is being invested in additional plant and machinery to create more wealth. The pre-industrial countries of Asia only have about £20 a head to live on, that is, for both consumption and production goods. The West is thus saving more than the East is spending on everything. No wonder that the gap in wealth between the West and Asia is steadily widening. Moreover, most new scientific and technical discoveries or developments tend to widen the gap still more just because the already rich countries have the capital to make full use of them, but the poor countries have not.

from the Presidential Address to the 119th Annual Conference of the British Association for the Advancement of Science (1957)

PROFESSOR P. M. S. BLACKETT

What seem to be the richest areas in the world? What seem to be the poorest?

Which of the two areas has the highest population and how much larger is it?

How much money per head per year has the richest area?

How much money per head per year has the poorest area?

What interesting fact does the writer present about the previous standard of living in some of the poorer countries?

What has recently happened in certain countries to make them so much richer than all the rest of the world?

Why is it that in those countries where the majority of the population is engaged in agriculture, it seems impossible to increase the national prosperity?

What is the effect on agriculture when a country becomes industrialized?

What must happen in a country if the scientific and technological advances are to go on increasing its wealth?

128

Why is the gap in wealth between the rich and poor countries steadily widening?

Now that you know these facts, do you think there is any chance of solving this problem? Have you any solutions to offer?

A doctor from the U.S.S.R. goes to India

Olga Makeeva is a Russian who was asked by the World Health Organization of the United Nations to use her skills as a doctor to help some of the less fortunate people in the world.

Lying twenty-six kilometres from the nearest medical centre, the remote Indian village of Sohra was almost entirely without roads and could be reached only with the greatest difficulty. However, it would have been impossible to ignore that village. Two thousand five hundred people had their homes there, yet there were no medical facilities for maternity cases or for child care. The village council had no premises in which a medical centre could have been opened. In fact the only building suitable for this purpose belonged to the local temple. But the local Brahmin priest who served the goddess Medli had several times refused to hand over this building either to serve as a school or for medical purposes, justifying his decision by affirming that the goddess had always refused any such suggestion he had made to her. The Brahmin and I had a talk, and I asked him to speak once more to the goddess, this time in our name. He left me to petition the goddess again and returning at 11 o'clock at night, escorted by a large crowd of villagers, he reported to me the following news: 'You are lucky. The goddess has given you her blessing. You can take over the building and use it for any purpose you like.' In two weeks'

129

time, that same Brahmin attended the celebrations when we opened in the building a maternity centre with four beds, and it was he who invited the whole village to a dinner in honour of the occasion.

This was only one picturesque incident during my unforgettable two-year mission in India. I had been sent there by the World Health Organization as a gynaecologist, my assignment being to serve as senior expert and consultant and as the leader of a group of experts on maternal and child health. Our mission took us to the state of Saurashtra, which means 'good country', and is one of the states of western India. It contains 85 towns and 4,500 villages with a total population of four and a half million. The state includes a tropical forest, two hundred miles long, in the depths of which lions are still to be found. . . .

Saurashtra's Health Department was established in 1948, after India became independent. In its early days the department was chiefly engaged in the struggle against epidemics and such diseases as malaria, tuberculosis, etc., but in 1955 it extended its activities to cover maternal and child welfare. At this point, the government turned to the United Nations Children's Fund (UNICEF) and to the World Health Organization (WHO) for help. A plan was drawn up covering a period of two years. This provided for an increase of 350–700 in the number of hospital beds, the establishment in the towns of Rajkot, Bhaunagar and Junagadh of the first hundred children's beds ever made available in the state, the opening of twenty urban consulting rooms for women and children and of twenty-six village medical centres, with four maternity sub-centres, the starting of courses for two hundred women wishing to become midwives and of refresher courses for two hundred midwives already practising in the villages. WHO assigned two experts, one from the U.S.S.R. as senior consultant (myself), with general responsibilities, and the other Miss Catherine Walsh from the United Kingdom, who was responsible for the training of medical personnel. . . .

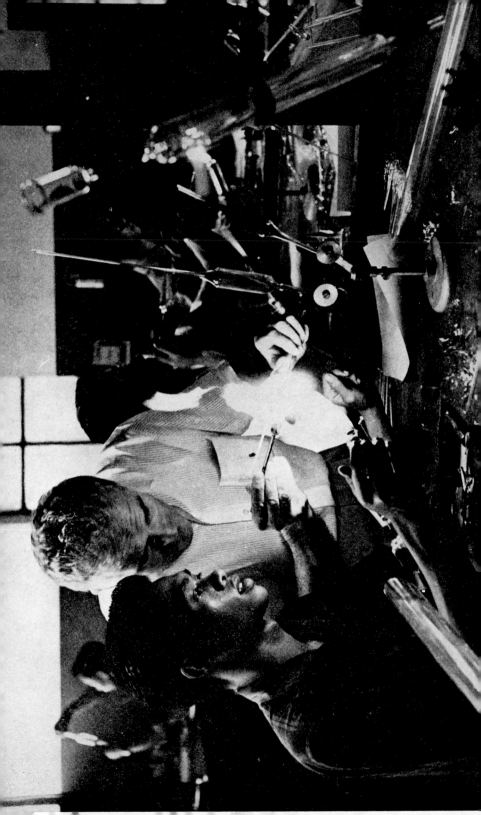

Although a government and the specialized agencies may be in a position to provide all the necessary material means and technical guidance, no health project can succeed until the people for whom it is intended understand its significance and take a conscious and active part in it. For this reason, we first made contact with the municipal authorities, with the village authorities, and with many Indian health organizations. . . . Our project was discussed from all angles at five regional conferences attended by medical workers as well as representatives of the local authorities and different organizations. . . .

Thanks to the support of the authorities and various organizations, Saurashtra's maternity and child care project was able to surpass the goal that had been set forth. In the towns, thirty consulting rooms for women and children were opened, instead of the twenty originally planned, while in the villages 120 maternity sub-centres were in existence, where only fifty-two had been intended. By 1957, one-third of the inhabitants of Saurashtra were receiving qualified medical help for maternity cases. It is now clear that, with the help of the local authorities and the people themselves, complete obstetric service will be available, not in fifteen years as originally estimated, but when the second Indian Five-Year Plan comes to an end in 1961.

In two years a great task had been accomplished. The medical personnel had been trained in real understanding of the task which lies ahead and in a sense of responsibility for the duties incumbent on them. Every medical worker on the spot had his own individual duties in maternal and child care, based on the keeping of accurate records in every village of all women and children up to the age of five years and of all confinements.

Most of these medical workers in the villages approached their task with tremendous enthusiasm, and many of them worked miracles. For example, in the year 1957 in the village of Karedi, with three thousand inhabitants, the midwife Savita-ben attended 136 confinements, and in eight cases where complications occurred, she sent the patients away for treatment at the proper time. On one occasion, having a case of haemorrhage, she awoke the Maharanee in the middle of the night, borrowed her car and sent her patient in it to hospital, thus saving her life. Savita-ben's work did not come to an end with the delivery of the child. She also saw to it that all the local children up to one year old were vaccinated against smallpox. As the result of her work and that of her colleagues in 1957, 127 cases of complications were treated in time and the lives of all the mothers saved. The death rate among mothers in Saurashtra fell in 1957 to a quarter of what it had been and the number of stillbirths to one-third.

Women and Technical Assistance reprinted from

UNITED NATIONS REVIEW

Most communities wishing to make radical changes meet with difficulties. The Brahmin priest's refusal to hand over the building is a typical example. Why do you think the doctor handled the situation as she did without asking for government backing?

Why had the Saurashtra Health Department not tackled the problem of maternal welfare before 1955? What difficulties were they up against?

WHO were able to assign only two doctors to help four million people. In what way does this limit their role?

Why do you think the WHO doctors held so many conferences with various local organizations?

Why was a plan with target dates drawn up? Do you feel this helped the newly trained medical workers?

What strikes you about the way all kinds of people in Saurashtra responded to the maternal welfare scheme?

What strikes you about conditions in countries such as India? What else do you feel can be done to help the people living there? Do you think they should be helped?

CREATIVE WRITING

International co-operation does not make the headlines so easily as international friction. But a recent book or television programme may give you a clue to one of the many interesting ways in which nations are co-operating. Look up some more information and write a report for the class.

How do you think co-operation could help the world? Do young people get any chance to help? Is it fair to expect the better-off countries like our own to help the rest? Is it a good thing to disrupt a settled community, even though it is technically backward? These are just a few of the problems that arise. Think over and discuss one that disturbs, worries or attracts you, then put down your conclusions and describe how you arrived at them.

CODA

When we think with seriousness and honesty our opinions often change and sometimes our attitudes alter. Look back now at the past year. Would you say any of your attitudes have altered? Do you notice any personal changes in yourself? Have you new hopes and aspirations? Read again the poem 'Prayer before Birth'. How does it seem to you a year later?

When you have thought about these ideas, write something about yourself—a story, a poem, or just a piece in your own style. Something to keep and read when you are old and wondering what you were like as a young boy or girl growing into life.

In working on these themes we, the authors, have learnt a lot from our pupils about their ideas and experiences. If you have felt particularly satisfied with some piece of work you have written, we would be interested to read it. You can send it to us addressed to John Dixon, c/o The Clarendon Press, Oxford. Mark the name of this book clearly in the left-hand corner of the envelope.

The knowledge and insight of many of the following writers have been a great help in preparing this book. We, the authors, would like to thank them or their executors, and their publishers, for permission to use extracts from their books.

R. Allerton & T. Parker: *The Courage of His Convictions* (Hutchinson)
Brendan Behan: *Borstal Boy* (Hutchinson)
Antony Bertram: *Design* (Penguin Books Ltd)
Professor P. M. S. Blackett: Presidential Address to the British Association for the Advancement of Science, 1957
John Braine: *Room at the Top* (Eyre & Spottiswoode)
Sid Chaplin: *The Day of the Sardine* (Eyre & Spottiswoode)
Sir Winston Churchill: *The Second World War Vol. ii* (Cassell & Co. Ltd)
Winifred Elkin: *The English Penal System* (Penguin Books Ltd)
W. Faulkner: *Sanctuary* (Chatto & Windus Ltd and Random House, Inc.)
Maxim Gorky: *My Childhood* (Foreign Languages Pub. House, Moscow)
Margaret Hill: *An Approach to Old Age* (Oliver & Boyd)
Hilde Himmelweit: *Television and the Child* (O.U.P. and Nuffield Foundation)
Richard Hoggart: *The Uses of Literacy* (Chatto & Windus Ltd)
Robert Jungk: *Children of the Ashes* (William Heinemann Ltd and Harcourt, Brace & World, Inc.)
Arthur Koestler: *Darkness at Noon* (Jonathan Cape Ltd)
Philip Larkin: 'Toads' from *The Less Deceived* (The Marvell Press)
D. H. Lawrence: *Sons and Lovers, Selected Essays* (By permission of L. Pollinger Ltd, and the estate of the late Mrs Frieda Lawrence)
Louis Macneice: Stanzas from 'Prayer Before Birth' (Faber & Faber Ltd)
Albert Maltz: *The Journey of Simon McKeever* (Victor Gollancz Ltd)
Margaret Mead: *Growing up in New Guinea* (Routledge & Kegan Paul and William Morrow & Company Inc.), © 1930 by M. Mead
Wright Mills: *White Collar Girl* (O.U.P.)
George Orwell: *Selected Essays* (Martin Secker & Warburg Ltd)
Siegfried Sassoon: 'Counter Attack', *Collected Poems* (Faber & Faber Ltd)
Alan Sillitoe: *Saturday Night and Sunday Morning* (W. H. Allen)
Muriel Spark: *The Go Away Bird* (Punch and Macmillan)
Susan Stebbing: *Thinking to Some Purpose* (Penguin Books Ltd)
H. S. Turner: *Something Extraordinary* (Michael Joseph Ltd)
Richard Wright: *Black Boy* (Victor Gollancz Ltd)
Extracts from 'Rebuilding Britain' by permission of the Royal Institute of British Architects. 'Family Viewing' by permission of The Council for Children's Welfare. 'Sicilian Documents' from *The New English Review* (Halcyon Press Ltd). *The United Nations Review*. *Which?* (Consumers' Association Ltd). *The Daily Express*. *The Sketch*. *The Times*.

Essays and Exercises

Essay Suggestions

Imaginative

1. A lonely old lady (or old man) looks out from behind her curtain and watches the people in the street. Describe what she sees and what she thinks.
2. An old man looks back on the district he lives in and talks about how it used to look fifty years ago and the changes he has seen.
3. Grandmother comes to the rescue in a family quarrel.

Argumentative

1. Would you say the old age pensioner is fairly treated? Justify your opinion and say what changes, if any, you think should be made.
2. Should old people stop work at 65? Justify your opinion and explain the reasons for and against.
3. Are old people less understanding of the young than young people are of the old?

General

1. Interview two or three old people that you know, and find out what they need and enjoy most, and whether they get it.
2. What do you feel most towards old people?—pity, admiration, scorn, affection . . .? Describe two or three old people you know well and show which feelings come uppermost.
3. Do you know of any old people who take an active part in the life of the family or of the community? Describe them and what they do.

Facts and Exercises

a. Write a paragraph giving five things for teenagers to remember when living with old people.

b. Describe in one or two paragraphs the furnishings of an old-fashioned room.

c. Two old cronies meet again. Report their conversation.

d. Write a letter thanking your grandparents for having you to stay.

e. List briefly five ways in which you feel old people can best be helped by the young.

f. (i) Find the current statistics for old age pensions, tabulate them, and explain in a paragraph how you would have to budget on a pension.

    (ii) Find out how a pension scheme works.

PARENTS AND CHILDREN

Essay Suggestions

Imaginative

1. The family out visiting compared and contrasted with the family on Monday morning.
2. The family setting out or returning from holiday.
3. Bringing home the first boy or girl friend.
4. Your father takes you to your first soccer match.
5. The new baby arrives.

Argumentative

1. How should parents educate their children about sex?
2. The advantage and disadvantages of being an only child as against living in a large family.
3. Working mothers—advantages and disadvantages.

General

1. A TV family: is it phoney or true to life?
2. Happy moments for your mother and father (ask them!).
3. What happens to children when the family breaks up?
4. The changing problems that parents face as their children grow up.

Facts and Exercises

a. Explain in a paragraph of five sentences:
   why you were late home;
   why, according to your father, he can't give you more pocket money;
   why, according to your mother, you should keep your room tidy.

b. Describe in one or two paragraphs:
   your family watching TV;
   helping clean the car or decorate;
   helping your mother wash up or clean.

c. Report a family conversation:
   round the breakfast table;
   when Dad comes back from work;
   at the seaside.

d. Write a letter home reassuring your parents about your safety on a first holiday without them.
   Write a letter from a mother to her married daughter, trying tactfully to point out that she is spoiling the baby.

e. List briefly five rules for parents of teenagers or for teenagers in the home.

f. Find statistics on the size of families (with children) in Great Britain. Show how the facts should affect plans for housing.

THE HOME

Essay Suggestions

Imaginative

1. Describe a personality by describing his or her room.
2. Living with in-laws.
3. Moving from an old slum to a new flat.

Argumentative

1. Which is preferable: an old spacious house or a small modern flat?
2. Do too many families try to keep up with the Joneses when furnishing and decorating their houses?
3. Discuss the merits of various combinations of dining, living and kitchen space. Illustrate the problems.

General

1. The housewife and her home.
2. Kitchens old and new.
3. Children in flats.
4. How to plan a room of one's own on a limited budget. Illustrate with diagrams.
5. Discuss and criticize some ideal colour scheme for a home.

Facts and Exercises

a. Explain in a paragraph how the layout round the kitchen sink can reduce work and strain for the housewife.
b. (i) In one paragraph give brief instructions on wallpapering, or painting woodwork.
   (ii) Describe an overcrowded breakfast table or overcrowded room.
c. Report a dialogue:
   between parents discussing decorating or replanning;
   between housewives discussing problems and deficiencies in their houses or flats.
d. Write a letter to your landlord asking him firmly but politely to deal with some repairs or improvements he has promised. Write a letter to a firm asking for samples of wallpaper patterns, furnishing patterns . . .
e. List briefly the things you think essential in a small bed-sitting-room for a teenage boy or girl.
f. Compile statistics on suitable sizes for rooms serving various purposes; on lighting, power points and electrical equipment needed; on size of windows, etc. Survey your own home and possibly one or two others; then compare the results, working in pairs.

THE NEIGHBOURHOOD

Essay Suggestions

Imaginative

1. An accident to a boy playing in the street.
2. The park seen through the eyes of a child and of an old lady.
3. A bunch of town boys out on a wild moor or mountain.

138

Argumentative

1. Where you would like to live, and why?
2. Are people less neighbourly in new flats and estates?
3. Which to choose: a semi-detached or a terrace or square.

General

1. Contrast an old slum area with a new estate.
2. The way life in your street or locality is affected by bad planning.
3. Improvements you would make to your street or area.

Facts and Exercises

a. Explain in a paragraph the five greatest problems of your area.
   Explain in a paragraph:
   how an area should be planned to meet children's needs;
   how it should be planned to meet teenagers' needs . . .
b. Describe an ugly or beautiful piece of 'street furniture' (say a bench, lamp-post, bus shelter).
c. Write a letter to the council:
   asking them to let a group of you carry out some useful alteration to your area;
   asking for some necessary social service to be provided;
   suggesting sensible improvements in your street.
d. List briefly the problems created by traffic and offer some solutions.
e. Collect statistics on the cost of various forms of social services in your area and compile charts of the various people and bodies involved.

WORK

Essay Suggestions

Imaginative

1. A nurse or miner or docker . . . starting their day's work or ending their day's work.
2. A visit to a factory, office or workshop (based on experience?).
3. The first morning at a new job.

Argumentative

1. What do you think is the best (or worst) kind of job to do and why?
2. Which jobs are most important, which fairly important, which unimportant—or are they all of importance, to society?
3. What is the point of having Unions in various trades and professions?

General

1. My week-end job.
2. An interview with a member of the family about his or her job.
3. The advice of a Youth Employment Officer on points to remember when choosing a career.

Facts and Exercises

a. Explain in a paragraph:
   five advantages or disadvantages of working in a factory;
   five important things to bear in mind when choosing a career.
b. Write a paragraph describing:
   a typist at work;
   a shopkeeper at work;
   a salesman, milkman, policeman . . .
c. Report a conversation:
   at tea-break in the factory or office;
   in a doctor's surgery . . .
d. Write a letter:
   applying for further information about a job that has been advertised;
   turning down an offer of a job (made by a well-intentioned relative of yours).
e. List five important rights of young people at work (see Factory Acts).
f. Collect statistics and information on the pay and prospects for a group of trades, crafts, professions . . .

ADVERTISEMENTS

Essay Suggestions

1. Write a detailed criticism of a longer advertisement (try baldness cures, motor-car tyres, or patent medicines, for example); look for vague wording, exaggerated claims, misleading suggestions and any other methods of persuasion.
2. After your class discussion on 'What adverts. do' write a summary of the main conclusions. Support each of your points by a small, well-chosen advert. cut out from a current newspaper or magazine.
3. Think of a new product and draft two advertisements, one reasonable the other not, for inclusion in a good teenage or school magazine.
4. Analyse a pictorial or television advertisement.
5. How far do people take notice of advertisements for new products? Choose a suitable product and survey some of your friends or neighbours to find out how they have reacted to the advertising; then write up a brief report on your efforts.
6. Write a report for your form on the work done by Consumers' Association's magazine, *Which?* (obtainable in most libraries).
7. As the family watches TV the adverts. come on. Describe how they all react and imagine an argument or discussion.
8. A realistic picture of a persuasive and unscrupulous salesman at work. Imagine him calling on your mother.

Facts and Exercises

a. Write five sentences on:
    a good advertisement
    a misleading advertisement
describing it and giving the reasons why it is good or bad.
b. Write one or two paragraphs showing how an advert. is made attractive to us.
c. Write a conversation between two housewives discussing a widely advertised product they are dissatisfied with.
d. Write a letter complaining about a misleading advert. or asking for additional information about a new product recently advertised.
e. List briefly five things a good advertisement should contain.

141

f. Study the newspapers, billboards, etc., and report briefly on what other things, besides manufactured products, are advertised, commenting on what you find.

NEWSPAPERS

Essay Suggestions

1. Imagine you are a reporter. Write up a local news item, using headings and sub-headings, on:
    (*a*) a crash (quoting eye-witness accounts). Try to establish what actually happened.
    (*b*) the opening of a new store or starting of a new housing development, etc.
    (*c*) a local man or woman who has won a championship or is starting out on a journey round the world.
    (*d*) an interesting local industry.
2. Write about one of these people from any aspect you like.
    (*a*) The street corner newspaper seller.
    (*b*) A boy on a newspaper round.
    (*c*) The editor.
3. Choose two passages reporting the same event but written from different standpoints, e.g. a Soccer report; a debate in Parliament. Discuss the way each writer has selected some facts while omitting others and show the way the language used gives a slant to what is reported.

Facts and Exercises

a. Write a paragraph making five points of criticism or appreciation of newspapers.
b. (i) Select a newspaper picture that effectively adds something to a written report. Describe the picture in one or two paragraphs and explain its use.
    (ii) Describe in one or two paragraphs an effective political or social cartoon, by Giles, Low, Vicky, etc., showing how it makes its point.

c. Write a conversation between:
  (i) a reporter and an unreliable and gossipy eye-witness;
  (ii) a person who thinks an article of news is true and some-
      one who will not believe a word of it.
d. Write a letter to a newspaper:
  (i) disagreeing with a point of view expressed in an article;
  (ii) giving more facts about an incident that was reported.
e. List the main national newspapers according to the political
    parties they support.
f. Find out which newspapers are read by several of your friends
    and neighbours, and how many different newspapers each one
    reads. Find the circulation figures for the national daily
    newspapers. Make any comment on what you have discovered.

COMICS AND MAGAZINES

Essay Suggestions

1. Describe some of the best-known heroes or heroines of the
   comics and discuss how phoney or true to life they are.
2. An off-beat story for teenagers (draw on your own experience,
   not stock situations).
3. Analyse a comic or magazine and suggest improvements you
   would like to see.
4. Compare two comics or magazines of the same type, showing
   how one is better than the other.
5. An article for teenagers, e.g. about clothes for a seaside holiday (and not just following the fashion!).
6. Compare a comic classic with the original.
7. What I should like to see in a (general) magazine for teenagers—and why.

Facts and Exercises

a. A paragraph of five points of contrast between two comics or
    two magazines.
b. (i) A paragraph giving five reasons why I still (or no longer)
        read comics.
   (ii) A paragraph describing several types of villain or
        hero(ine).

(iii) A paragraph stating five reasons for recommending a good magazine.
c. Parody the dialogue of a magazine situation you dislike.
d. Reply to a letter you disagree with in a hobby or current affairs magazine.
e. List five things you would like to see eliminated or improved in a magazine you know, giving your reasons.
f. Make a summary of the main points in a series of readers' letters on one subject.

TELEVISION

Essay Suggestions

1. An evening with the family watching television.
2. The family discusses a programme.
3. A television interview.
4. Behind the camera.
5. Compare two similar programmes: consider personalities, treatment of subject, camera work, etc.
6. Why are Westerns so popular?
7. Are quiz programmes just a racket?
8. A programme I learnt something from.
9. Suggestions for improving B.B.C./I.T.V. programmes.
10. A balanced evening's viewing.

Facts and Exercises

a. Five points on a TV programme that you like.
b. A paragraph briefly reviewing a documentary or describing a TV character.
c. A discussion between two schoolchildren on a programme seen the previous evening.
d. Letter to B.B.C. or I.T.V. sending a complaint or congratulations on a programme.
e. List briefly the subjects you think TV tackles most successfully and comment.
f. A short TV script.